EXPERIMENTAL POP

EXPERIMENTAL POP

Frontiers of the Rock Era

BY BILLY BERGMAN AND RICHARD HORN

BLANDFORD PRESS
Poole • Dorset

First published in the U.K. 1985
by Blandford Press
Link House, West Street,
Poole, Dorset, BH15 1LL

A QUARTO BOOK

EXPERIMENTAL POP: Frontiers of the Rock Era
was produced and prepared by
Quarto Marketing Ltd.
15 West 26th Street New York, N.Y. 10010

British Library Cataloguing in Publication Data

Bergman, William
Experimental pop
William Bergman—(The Planet rock series: 2)
1. Music, Popular (Songs, etc.)—History
and criticism
I. Title II. Series
780'.42'0904 ML3470

ISBN 0-7137-1550-2

Editor: Karla Olson
Design: Lesley Achitoff
Photo Research: Susan Duane

Typeset by BPE Graphics, Inc.
Printed and bound in The United States by
The Maple-Vail Group

Cover photo by Paula Court
Color rendering by Sean Daly

BILLY BERGMAN, formulator and principal writer for the Planet Rock Series, has written on world music fusion in publications from the *EAST VILLAGE EYE,* to the Parisian *AUTREMENT.* Bergman lives in New York City, where he also writes scripts for short films and multimedia.

RICHARD HORN is the author of *ATTACHED*—a piece of audio-musical theater written in collaboration with Phil Kline of the Del-Byzanteens—and two plays with music, *IPANEMA* and *TWO CARTOGRAPHERS.* He has also written about design and architecture for numerous magazines, and is the author of *DESIGNS,* a novel, and *FIFTIES STYLE,* a book about American design in the 50s. Horn lives in New York City.

CONTENTS

PREFACE ix

INTRODUCTION xi

1 • EAST MEETS WEST 1

2 • NEW SOUNDS 19

3 • TAPESYNTH TECH 44

4 • NEW CONTEXTS 61

5 • PERFORMANCE 76

6 • SOUNDS FAMILIAR 99

BIBLIOGRAPHY 113

INDEX 115

PREFACE

There are new sounds entering all levels of Anglo-American music, from Top Forties pop to New Wave rock, to classical music. They can be heard in "All Night Long" by Lionel Richie, "Remain in Light" by the Talking Heads, "I'll Tumble 4 Ya" by Boy George's Culture Club, "Roxanne" by the Police, and "Satyagraha" by Philip Glass. There's a certain bounciness, a driving repetition, a disruption of regular rhythms—or more precisely, the latest wave of Caribbean, Latin, and African infusions influencing "First World" music.

In the early 80s, American and British record giants faced sagging sales figures and blamed home taping and Pac-Man. Only recently have they admitted the possibility that their audiences may be bored with the "corporate rock sound of REO Speedwagon, Styx, and all those groups you can't tell apart without a scorecard," as one record exec put it. New classical music, considered inaccessible to most listeners, was not even distributed by major labels.

Meanwhile, rich new fusions in music have been forming. The cross-pollenization of musical ideas, which for millenia has spread from region to region along paths of peddlers and displaced peoples, has, within recent decades, been furiously speeded up with the help of new technology. Tape recording, world air travel, and globe-wide radio broadcasting have only recently come into existence. Even newer is the near universality—at least in urban areas—of electrical outlets that accommodate the plugs of electric guitar amps and public-address systems.

Japanese box radios blare the Rolling Stones in the markets of Colombia; local boys play imitations of James Brown in the dance halls of Dakar. Perhaps traveling even greater musical distances, a classical composer can listen to rock on a Walkman. The phenomenon causes musicologists to dispair over the loss of traditional and classical musical styles. French cultural ministers rant about the dominance of Anglo-American pop garbage on world airways.

It would be sad if the variety of music now present in the world did grind down to the bland version of American pop played by Menudo. But if world musical activity of the past ten years is any indication, that won't happen. Cross-pollenizations are as rich as they sound; new hybrids of music have been breeding all over the globe, true to the spirit of local traditions and fully utilizing the emotional and structural forces behind those traditions. Bandleaders and composers everywhere are taking advantage of the new tools and techniques available to them—the rumble of the electric bass, the push-button sound waves of synthesizers, the pastiche possiblilities of the multitrack recording studio, and rhythms and timbres learned from faraway music. And some revolutionary new sounds are coming out: electronic juju and merengue bands, Brazilian "tropicalista" samba rock, reggae, soca, white-noise rock, high-volume art "trance" music, and the so-called "New Music" (as the music industry is calling rock with the new rhythms, such as the music of the Police), which is revitalizing rock. The rapid development and proliferation of these styles doesn't lessen the pleasure they offer. In fact, it is the freshness of these juxtapositions that is most appealing in the raw fusions of styles and surprising combinations of instruments. Sweet vocal lines meet turbulent drumming; pianos are accompanied by gourds.

In the mid-60s, when bluesmen Howlin' Wolf and Muddy Waters toured Europe with groups such as the Rolling Stones and the Yardbirds, rock was invigorated by this exposure to its roots. But blues also benefited from the exchange—it became a powerful presence on the world music scene. In the late 70s and into the 80s, catalytic agents such as Malcolm McLaren and Brian Eno have been schooling rock groups in third-world rhythms and experimental textures. They see that the world is too small for popular audiences to be kept from the source founts of this new invigoration. In music today, reggae has already swept the world outside its island home. With worldwide record sales of amazing volume—$240 million to date—Bob Marley and the Wailers easily sold out stadiums holding up to 100,000 people on nearly every continent before Marley's early death in 1981. Jimmy Cliff, Peter Tosh, and a host of other singers, and disc jockeys such as Yellowman continue to hold world attention, making cult films as well as hit records.

Latin American music, the constant shaker of jazz, has crossed seas and isthmi in dozens of dance crazes over the last 60 years. Now it is threatening to take over American and European nightlife, with the popularity of Brazilian nightclubs multiplying in the last few years.

King Sunny Adé and his eighteen African Beats, flown straight from Lagos on a special deal with Nigerian Airways, sold out 4,000 person concert halls around the world. With a roiling texture of traditional Yoruba and electric instruments, they spurred hours of dancing from first-time listeners and sparked media exultation in nationwide publications from *Newsweek* to *Penthouse*. The *Village Voice* hailed King Sunny Adé as the successor to Bob Marley, "on his way to becoming the first truly international star in the history of pop."

Laurie Anderson broke out of the New York downtown art scene with a hit single in Britain, followed by a Warner Brothers contract and worldwide tours of her "United States" opus. Her concerts usually were received by standing ovations from audiences made up of people from every category of music lover; New Wave enthusiasts to opera subscription holders.

Crossovers such as these will be increasingly important in the popular music scene in the years to come, obvious by the excitement they've produced in the recording industry and among the general public. The *Planet Rock* series is an introduction to the performers of this new sonic world. The first volume covers Latin and Caribbean pop; the second volume, here, examines the dynamic merging of experimental music and the pop sensibility; and the third volume takes an in-depth look at the new popular music emerging in Africa. None of these works are meant to be an exhaustive guide to their subjects. The huge variety of emerging musics makes it difficult to include all categories or performers here. Hopefully these books will cause the reader to investigate further; they provide a springboard for the reader to take the plunge.

INTRO-DUCTION

Not too long ago—around 1970— if you were to walk into an avant-garde music concert anywhere in the United States or Europe, you'd probably be greeted by an austere stage graced with either a pair of speaker monoliths or a dour-looking chamber ensemble. After listening to bleeps, bloops, and scratches for a couple of hours you might have the same reaction that music critic David Ewen noticed at the time. He said audiences reacted like "Red" Buttons in a routine from his TV show: "From time to time he would cup his hands over his ears, cock his head to one side while his eyes sparkled with hidden laughter, and exclaim: 'Strange things are happening!' "

Danbury Scott-Fanton Museum and Historical Society

Charles Ives at age sixteen, fulfilling his father's experimental dreams: A portrait of the artist as a budding rugged individualist.

Well, strange things are still happening in the world of avant-garde music, but lately, popular audiences have begun to take their hands away from their ears. Avant-garde or experimental "art" music—music from the classical tradition that explores new directions—has recently sprouted a branch that reaches out to the modern eardrum. Unlike earlier avant-garde music, this new music is part of the Rock Era, and uses a rhythmic drive and wide variety of new sonic material. In fact, it often sounds an awful lot like rock 'n' roll. At the same time, rock—usually a mass-market music more consumer-tested than composed—has been allowed to move further away from pat formulas, and sounds stranger and stranger, often resembling avant-garde music with its adventurous spirit, structure, and technique. Indeed, though it is traditionally believed that classical music and rock go together like boeuf bourguignonne and ice cream, main course and dessert have been drawing closer and closer, creating a whole new category of sonic nourishment (or sonic fast-food, depending on whom you ask). This new category could be called pop experimentalism, if a label is necessary and it can cover composers who come from both the rock world and the world of art music.

The reason that experimental art music and rock music have been affecting each other is not hard to understand. A generation of classically trained composers has grown up with the excitement of rock. And rock musicians left the backwoods and the ghettos long ago. Both camps have had ample opportunity to hear each other's music blaring from the same radios and the same standard LP discs. And now they go to the same parties and even to each other's concerts. "After the premiere of my *Octet,* a guy with white makeup came up to me back stage, introduced himself as Brian Eno, and told me how much he enjoyed the concert," said Steve Reich, a classically oriented experimentalist, recounting a now not uncommon experience. Reich continues: "It's a very good situation where the pop musicians and the classical musicians are basically rubbing elbows and are aware of each other and are influencing each other... I benefited from the rock world... I'm not going to pin down what I got, but I got a lot, and I'm glad if I can give something back. That's the situation now. That's what I love about rock music; that's what I love about Bach! Passacaglia and sarabande—that's popular dance! You hear a violin sonata and you can say: 'that's what I get at the club, that's what I hear when I get juiced. But oh, man, that's a classy job of doing it.' That's a healthy musical society! That's a good situation. And I think, that's what we're living in right now."

Rock and avant-garde music have been affected, not only by each other, but by the same inpouring of new stimuli: the waves of non-Western music that roll in as the world shrinks; the quick-changing technologies of multi-track studios, sound synthesis, amplification, and computers. Pop experimentalists, whether they are linked mainly to the rock scene or to the avant-garde, have developed the same thirst for new sounds, the same desire for the all-encompassing performance or—as it is called—opera, and the same desires to use new performance methods such as video.

It is with an eye on these various fields of interest that we have mapped out this book. We will discuss how composers, whether rock or classical or somewhere in-between, have responded to these new stimuli. Each new stimulus demands its own chapter. Philip Glass, Steve Reich, Laurie Anderson, Meredith Monk, and others, are bound to pop up in several places, for they have responded to a number of stimuli—certainly part of the reason that their music has enjoyed a great deal of success in the 80s. By introducing composers in several chapters, we hope to avoid lumping them into new categories, or legitimizing easy disposal of them into existing ones, such as "minimalism." We feel that these categories tend to dissolve once the music's many facets are taken into account. One of the most striking things about this music is its new audience, one that—like the music itself—defies easy categorization. Indeed, by 1981 *Life* magazine was able to announce (in an article about Philip Glass subtitled "Composing Classics from Raga and Rock") that "though hardly dance music, Glass' records are heard squeezed between the latest Blondie and Donna Summer's singles at many discos. The most fashionable punk clubs in New York are demanding Glass' group for their late-night shows. 'I got both blue hairs and pink hairs,' he says, 'There are no hierarchies anymore. We now know that the greatest songwriter of the sixties was not Ned Rorem [a conservative art music composer] but Paul Simon, and there is more interest in a Talking Heads album than in most serious music written today.'"

What was the earlier avant-garde of modern "art" music? And why did it become boring to young composers like Glass, who—despite that boredom—are still primarily on the art side of the mix?

Earlier avant-garde music came directly out of the crisis which European classical music suffered around the turn of the century. Late nineteenth-century romantics such as Gustav Mahler followed their emotional rapture so wildly that they ran rampant over the strict rules of form that had developed during the previous centuries. These rules included melodies that followed a certain pattern of development, rhythms that governed movements of a piece with the regularity of a metronome, and harmonies that excluded notes that were not related to the key of a piece. The romantics used chord progressions that led back to the central key, but during the piece they wandered further and further from the key, coming back for a finale that seemed like the end of a saga. They cared more about high drama than form. Richard Wagner, the most extreme of the romantics, wandered even further away, especially in his use of chromaticism—notes not related to the key previously established. In fact, *The Ring of the Neibelung* operas seem organized more like storm systems than music. But for musicians at the turn of the century, there could be no turning back—freedom from the constraints of classical forms had to be taken to its extreme.

Arnold Schoenberg, a Viennese admirer of Wagner, did just that. By 1910, Schoenberg's music had become completely atonal—in other words, he used any note he wanted, wherever he wanted it, without melodies as we know them. His music seemed like disconnected leaps and piles of notes. In this music, he took an adventurous step, but the alienated response of audiences and popular critics was immediate and nearly universal. At the 1907 premiere of Schoenberg's *Chamber Symphony No. 1*, the booing of the audience turned into a riot.

As this occurred in the early years of Freudianism, it is not surprising that a woman sued Schoenberg because she claimed she had become neurotic from hearing his music. A psychiatrist backed her up, saying it was possible to develop mental illness from atonal music. Critics, in turn, were relentless: "Schoenberg's tone poem is not just filled with wrong notes," wrote the German Ludwig Karpath. "It is a fifty-minute-long protracted wrong note. One deals here with a man either devoid of all sense or who takes his listeners for fools." An English critic in the *Morning Post* went further, saying, "Modern intellect has advanced beyond elementary noise. Schoenberg has not."

Schoenberg, his students, and his small loyal following believed in the direction his music was taking, but by World War I there was nowhere else to go; there is no chaos beyond chaos. To advance, a new ordering system was needed.

Schoenberg stopped publishing music for eight years, and when he emerged from his cocoon, he had developed the twelve-tone system of composition. The core of a twelve-tone piece is a "series"—or ordered set—of all twelve notes possible within an octave. All twelve notes must be used once, in a determined order that is different for each piece, before the series is repeated. As the piece develops, the series can be used backwards, upside down, and in other configurations. But the primary rule remains firm: no note can be repeated before all twelve notes in the series are used.

There is no doubt that this is an ordering system, but it is one that insures complete atonality. To achieve tonality and melody, it is essential that some notes are given more importance than others, and that some notes are left out altogether. Because twelve-tone or "serial" music strictly prohibits these omissions, it sounds atonal. And, though highly structured, it is a structure completely incomprehensible to most listeners. Don't even try to hear the series, for you won't be able to. The beauty of a Schoenberg serial piece is instead in its unbound emotionality, the highly personal choices in instrumentation, dynamics, rhythm, and, of course, in the daring of what Schoenberg was doing when he developed this new compositional technique.

Not all art music composers embraced serial music. But throughout the 30s and 40s, there were several European composers who revered the works of Schoenberg and his former pupils Alban Berg and Anton Webern, who together formed the so-called Second Viennese School. After World War II, American composers such as Elliott Carter began writing music related to Schoenberg's earlier atonal music. At the same time, in Europe, composers including France's Pierre Boulez and Germany's Karlheinz Stockhausen extended the ideas of the serial technique. The music of both these offshoots was extremely complex and attracted few listeners. Nevertheless, it became *the* compositional techniques for art music composers in Europe (though not in the Soviet Union, where they were deemed symptoms of Western bourgeois decadence) and the United States.

But, by the 1950s, serial music had lost its freshness. It had become what Schoenberg himself never wanted it to become: mainstream art music, with total serialization championed by Boulez and the American Milton Babbitt. In their brand of serialism, all aspects of a piece of music—its rhythm, harmony, instrumentation, etc.—were determined by mathematically calculated systems along with the series of those twelve notes. Serialism became the method of composition as it was taught—and is still taught—in universities. But it was—and still is—a religion without a congregation, never having attracted even a small popular audience. And by the 60s many young composers found it stifling. For instance, Philip Glass, who had been composing serial pieces in Paris, looked around himself in Boulez's *Domaine Musicale* concert series and saw, "a wasteland, dominated by these maniacs, these creeps, who were trying to make everyone write this crazy, creepy music."

But the serialist route was not the only one in the twentieth century. There were individual experimentalists, conscious of the popular music of their time, who provided the models for composers who wanted to escape serialism, and to draw on more than just experimental art music traditions, but on pop traditions as well. Charles Ives was the most important of these role models, because of the breadth of his experimentation and his love of popular music. He composed most of his works from the turn of the century into the 20s, but was first recognized and had his music played by orchestras in the 50s and 60s.

Ives' father, George, was the bandmaster of the First Connecticut Heavy Artillery during the Civil War. George Ives, himself, was eager to investigate unexplored territory in music, but his job didn't give him much freedom. As General Grant said to President Lincoln when the president asked him whether or not he liked the music at one of Ives Senior's concerts, "I only know two tunes. One of them is Yankee Doodle. The other isn't." With such an unreceptive audience, Ives primed his son to do the experimenting. He taught him how to play a few instruments, about classical theory, and also taught him the popular songs of the time, like those of Stephen Foster ("Camptown Races," etc.).

Charles played the organ at his local church in Danbury, Connecticut, and the drums in his father's band. George led Charles through exercises in which he took material from popular music and did things with it that had never been done before. He would play two different songs in clashing keys on the piano at the same time; or would play "Jeanie With the Light Brown Hair" in one key and the accompaniment in another. The purpose of these games was to get Charles to appreciate dissonance—harmonies that sound jarring to the normal ear but are actually more interesting than sweet-sounding harmonies, because there is a greater variety to them.

Sometimes, George Ives would take Charles to a parade and emphasize the mixture of sounds as one band was marching away and one was coming toward them. George would divide his own band into groups that played from different corners of a town square, and then stand in the middle with his son and study the resulting sound. He had Charles listen to clumps of neighboring notes on a piano because they are somewhere in the cracks between keys and can only be played on a violin or sung—notes that are now called "microtones."

Charles Ives took all the material his father gave him—pop and classical, familiar and unfamiliar, old and new—and composed symphonies, art songs, and pieces completely his own. They were often created for ensembles never assembled before. *Steeples and Mountains,* for example, is for differently tuned sets of chimes and church bells playing with four trumpets and four trombones. Some pieces were written for ensembles that were never likely to get together, such as two marching bands approaching from different directions. There were four symphonies and many song cycles that collage popular music into a classical form. Ives' *114 Songs,* one of the few collections published during his lifetime, had a preface which summed up his attitude toward freewheeling experimentation and its connection to beauty in music: "A song has a few rights, the same as other ordinary citizens. . . . If it happens to feel like trying to fly where humans cannot fly, to sing what cannot be sung, to walk in a cave on all fours, to tighten up its girth in blind hope and faith and try to scale mountains that are not, who shall stop it?"

But, Ives was different from today's pop experimentalists in at least one important aspect: he never tried to make a living from his music, but worked all his life in the insurance business. He never tried to reach a wide audience; in fact, he tried to squelch any dissemination of his music beyond his personal friends. That's why most of his works have not been heard until the last few decades.

While Ives enforced his isolation, however, another American composer was dedicating himself to opening up the ears of the whole world. John Cage, born into a highly cultured family in Los Angeles in 1912, studied classical piano in the U.S. and Paris, but became interested in serialism and camped outside Schoenberg's door when the latter came to the U.S. in 1933. Cage composed twelve-tone music for six years, but at the same time became interested in the possibilities offered by Edgard Varèse (1883-1965), who composed entire works out of noises not usually thought of as musical—wails, metallic clangs, and tone clusters, for example. From his studies and experimentation, Cage saw rhythm as the essential bond to bring all these new ingredients together, and composed with everything from twelve-tone rows to cricket calls in an attitude he called "rhythmed sounds." He shoved screws, cloth, and boxes into pianos for many works of "prepared piano" music. He orchestrated the everyday sounds of a family home in a work called *Living Room.* He gradually realized that all the sounds and silences of the world are music, and that it is the job of the composer to sensitize audiences to those sounds. Cage made the most extreme statement of this concept in 1952 in a piece called *4'33"*. The score was originally written for the piano, but could be adapted for any instrument or combination of instruments. The piece lasts four minutes and thirty-three seconds, as the title implies, and the main instruction directing the performer is a marking of "tacet," which means that the performer plays nothing for the duration. No sounds come out of the piano, but Cage has carefully defined the time and situation of the piece. Any outside sound or silence occurring during that time becomes part of the composition. Cage asks his listeners to stretch their ears, to appreciate everything as music, even if it is not within the great Bach-Beethoven-Wagner-Schoenberg definitions of classical music.

Serious composers such as Philip Glass, searching for a way out of serialism in the 60s, took a cue from Ives and Cage and stretched their ears. But what did they hear? One thing they could not help but hear was the Big Beat. As *Time* magazine blared in 1965, "The big beat is everywhere. It resounds over TV and radio, in saloons and soda shops, fraternity houses, and dance halls. It has become, in fact, the international anthem of a new and restless generation. . . ."

The big beat is, of course, that of rock 'n' roll. Its strong pulse has been rock 'n' roll's essence since it began, as deejay Allan Freed demonstrated when he pounded a telephone book to the beat of the songs on his original "Moondog's Rock'n'Roll Party" radio show in 1952. And it's the driving, danceable rhythm of rock—the modern day passacaglia and sara-

CBS Records

Composer Edgard Varèse: His lifelong obsession was the "liberation of sound."

bande—that young composers such as Glass and Reich found missing in serial music.

In fact, classical music's connection with dance had become very weak by the late-nineteenth century. Instead, European art music (especially symphonic music) became so densely textured and over-orchestrated that its pulse seemed to have vanished completely. Some composers of the early twentieth century did attempt to restore that pulse. Certainly the most important of these was Igor Stravinsky. Born into a cultured and wealthy Russian family in 1882, Stravinsky first made a splash in Paris with three scores created for impresario Serge Diaghilev's Ballets Russes: *The Firebird* in 1910, *Petrouchka* in 1911; and, most significant of all, *The Rite of Spring* in 1913. An evocation of pagan Russia, *The Rite of Spring* featured ostinato—poundingly rhythmic, repeating melodic fragments—that shocked the Parisian audience at its premiere and incited a riot. To any rock fan hearing *The Rite of Spring* for the first time today, those rhythms would not be surprising. But in 1913, it seemed the sound of all hell breaking loose. While its sonorities were as big and rich as many late-nineteenth-century symphonic works, *The Rite of Spring* was far more—as we say today—"danceable." (In fact, the ballet climaxes when a virgin dances herself to death.) No one had ever heard anything like it before—and art music was never the same again.

Taking their cue from Stravinsky, several European art-music composers offered powerfully rhythmic compositions of their own between 1910 and the early 20s. Among them were Bela Bartók's *The Miraculous Mandarin,* Serge Prokofiev's *Scythian Suite* and Darius Milhaud's *L'Homme et son Desir.* At around the same time in Czechoslovakia, composer Leos Janàček, in

Igor Stravinsky, throughout his long career, made Western classical music pulse with complex rhythms.

Snowdon/Camera Press/Photo Trends

John Cage, pioneering avant-gardiste, serves his audience the musical sounds of everyday life.

Paula Court

works like the *Sinfonietta,* employed ostinato effects in his own highly original way, one that owed more to Czech folk music than to Stravinsky's revolutionary rhythms.

By the mid-20s, most European composers, including Stravinsky, had stopped writing for huge orchestral forces. Instead, they scored their works for chamber ensembles or small orchestras. But despite the reduced forces, the rhythmic drive of pieces like *The Rite of Spring* remained a primary characteristic of Stravinsky's music throughout his long life (he died in 1971). Interestingly enough, the link between rock and his own musical roots didn't go unnoticed by the composer himself. As John Miller Chernoff writes in a footnote to his book *African Rhythm and African Sensibility,* " 'The three Bs,' Stravinsky is said to have explained, 'are Bach, Beethoven, and Brown—James Brown.' "

But if rock's rhythmic drive was noted by innovative composers, rock 'n' roll itself was not open to experimentation until the late 60s. In the 50s, demanding fans liked sincerity and authenticity, applauding music that was true to its origins—black blues and poor white country—and true to the emotional intensity of these origins. Johnny Ray, for example (one of the earliest identifiable proto-rock 'n' rollers), when down on his knees sobbing "Cry," was celebrated by devotees as being more sincere than Elvis Presley on his third and fourth albums, with his more stylized, heavily orchestrated sounds.

But even sincere fans didn't seem to care about innovation in those halcyon days. Instead, by the late 50s, a rock "norm" had been established. Almost all the period's songs could have been cut from the same cookie cutter: they followed the blues chord progressions strictly, alternated chorus and verse in predictable patterns, included short boogie or blues instrumental solos, and usually lasted about three minutes—a convenient duration for interruption by radio commercials and for the maximization of jukebox income. Even as late as 1964, with the first wave of British rock, little could change this basic formula. Musically, in their early days of stardom, the Beatles and the Rolling Stones were merely reinjecting rock 'n' roll with a blues intensity and a note of British charm and humor—nothing too experimental.

Soon, though, the 1960s became "The Sixties," a culture and an attitude that extended far beyond the music. "Self-realization," "personal expression," and "freedom" were the catchwords of the new youth culture that looked toward rock music for its anthems. Authenticity in rock 'n' roll (now called by the more expansive name "rock") meant more than just "playin' the blues and playin' them right"—it meant "doing your own thing." A desire for experimentation became the order of the day.

But to do your own thing in commercial music, *you* have to control your means of production and distribution. As far as executives of large record companies are concerned, innovation is the last concern in marketing a record. For that reason, only a supergroup such as the Beatles could open rock up to experimentation. By 1967, the Beatles were making enough money to buy a small country if they had wanted to—let alone start their own record company. And they were able to hire one of the most creative producers and studio masters of the time, George Martin. With Martin's expertise and four-track recording equipment, their every whim became reality, and Beatlemania guaranteed it would sell. So, if George Harrison wanted to play a sitar on *Rubber Soul,* he could do it. And if the Fab Four felt like adding brass and violins, backward tape noises, and other electronic tricks to *Revolver,* who would stop them? And if Martin (who himself played in a brass band on Sundays in St. James' Park) suggested they do a song with a marching band theme, and if, as Martin reported, Paul McCartney said "Why don't we make the whole album as though the Pepper Band really existed, as though Sergeant Pepper was doing the record? We can dub in effects and things," then they could embark on the project,the musical personification of *Sergeant Pepper's*

Lonely Heart's Club Band, that turned rock into a style that encompassed a multitude of possibilities.

Charles Ives probably would have loved the *Sergeant Pepper* album. Under the unifying structure of the marching-band concept, it collages musical styles from raga to Tin Pan Alley. It includes a lot of dissonance and other strange sounds, the results of techniques Ives didn't have the technology to use, such as *musique concrete,* the collaging of real sounds recorded on tape. Not that the Beatles themselves were necessarily directly influenced by Ives. "I just shove a lot of sounds together, then shove some words on," John Lennon told Beatles chronicler Hunter Davies.

The actual creative process seems to have been a collaboration between the whims of the Beatles and the ingenuity of Martin. When Lennon wanted a circusy, hurdy-gurdy effect in "Being for the Benefit of Mr. Kite," he took steam organ sounds recorded on tape, cut the tape into irregular lengths, threw the pieces up in the air, and picked them off the floor, splicing them together at random. And much effort was spent to obtain dissonant noise fields. For the finale of "A Day in the Life," which was the finale of the record itself, John wanted "a sound building up from nothing to the end of the world." For this, a no-holds-barred gala was held at the Abbey Road studios in London. A 41-piece orchestra was hired; friends and celebrities were invited, including Mick Jagger and Marianne Faithful ; carnival costumes were given out—a famous violinist wound up in a gorilla suit, others wore peacock feathers and Asian robes. Tinted smoke filled the room, completing the exotic carnival atmosphere. George Martin told the orchestra the highest and lowest notes to be played; within that range it was a free-for-all, and the party lasted until 3 A.M. The cacophony created was the final crescendo, which in the album is topped off by a resounding piano chord extended with echo. Finally, there's a note at 20,000 hertz which only dogs can hear.

The release of the album, *Sergeant Pepper's Lonely Heart's Club Band* in June 1967 was hailed as "a decisive moment in the history of western civilization," by critic Kenneth Tynan, and as "a new and golden renaissance of song," by the *New York Times.* The Beatles had confirmed that rock, like art music, could be a vessel for musical experimentation and that people would accept it.

The immediate extension of this freewheeling rock experimentation was psychedelic rock. *Sergeant Pepper,* with its dreamlike, sometimes nightmarish dissonances, its surreal images, its song titles like "Lucy in the Sky with Diamonds," and its marijuana plants growing on the cover, came to be known as "psychedelic." Soon the Rolling Stones and the Who put out their own psychedelic discs. In San Francisco, where a good portion of the population was barely able to see straight, a slew of bands dedicated themselves to reproducing chemically altered inner fantasies: The Jefferson Airplane, The Grateful Dead, Moby Grape, Quicksilver Messenger Service, and Big Brother and the Holding Company were among the most famous. The three-minute jukebox song was shattered by the amps, stacked in towers stories high, with peak volumes three times that of the decade before, that filled listeners' heads with a dense barrage of sound. To reproduce the LSD experience, visuals as well as sound were needed; a complete environment, or total theater, was created in such venues as the Filmore in San Francisco. A similar club in New York, the Electric Circus, explained its light show: "This is an environment. It's like the advent of Feelys in *Brave New World*. Maybe we could show Nassau and program the sea smell and soft breezes. With five senses you learn more than with two senses. With five senses, it's happening. Our motto comes from the novelist Hermann Hesse: 'We are in a magic theater, a world of pictures not reality/Tonight at the magic theater for madmen only/the price of admission your mind.' " Songs would be extended for hours in the vague time-sense of an acid trip, and the blues and modal improvisations were boring unless you were in the proper ecstasy brought on by the whole mind-blowing experience. Jimi Hendrix made a guitar express the full heights of that ecstasy, and when it couldn't go far enough, he burnt it up on stage; Peter Townshend of the Who apparently had the same frustrations and began smashing his guitars. And rock as a music/theater spectacle flourished.

Meanwhile, outside of the mainstream, there were three musicians feeding off the excitement and craziness of 60s rock, who would later become inspirational models for rock ex-

perimenters: Frank Zappa and Captain Beefheart on the West Coast, and the Velvet Underground in New York. Frank Zappa was in his early twenties when the British Invasion started, and was already running his own "Studio Z" recording operation in Cucamonga, California. By 1966, when he formed the Mothers of Invention, he had an unusual mastery of the recording studio and—turning the rock of his time inside out—was able to go far beyond the strange sounds and collages of any commercial superstars. *Freak Out,* the Mothers' first album, has a percussive noise build-up worthy of Varèse, and *We're Only in it for the Money* dealt *Sergeant Pepper* and its hip American enthusiasts a satirical blow while at the same time outdoing its target in collage and electronic experiments. Sometimes collaborating with Zappa and the Mothers was Captain Beefheart (Don Van Vliet), who added the dimensions of dissonance and complex rhythm on his own LP *Trout Mask Replica.* Beefheart growled out blues in a Wolfman Jack voice and the sounds got so weird that he asked his record company to send a tree surgeon to make sure that a tree outside the house where he was rehearsing was not getting sick from the music.

The Velvet Underground was born in 1965 in the midst of the burgeoning New York art scene. In fact, it grew out of Andy Warhol's rock band called Exploding Plastic Inevitable. The original Velvet Underground included a classically trained musician—John Cale, who was schooled in viola at the Royal Conservatory of Music in London, and studied composition with art music heavies, Aaron Copeland and Iannis Xenakis, at Tanglewood in Massachusetts. He also studied with a New York composer named LaMonte Young, who had been developing a style later called minimalism—music that used very few notes, and repeated them, with slight variations, over and over, or held them for long periods of time like a drone. This corresponded with the minimalist aesthetic, one that favored a detached, logical approach to painting and sculpture, that was popular in the New York art world at the time. Minimalist artists such as sculptor Walter DeMaria would often sit in on Velvet Underground sets. The music the band played was minimal, pared down to just the essence of rock. It was sinewy, driving, and loud, with a large dose of extra-musical noise in the form of fuzz and feedback. This was the sound that would continue with Television, the New York

David Redfern/Retna Ltd.

The Beatles, in a still from *The Magical Mystery Tour Film,* opened rock to avant-garde techniques.

Dolls, the Sex Pistols, and the Ramones, becoming the prototype of punk, New Wave, and noise rock.

With so much experimentation occuring in the rock world, it was almost inevitable that art music's own mavericks would interest the more adventurous rockers. While Charles Ives and John Cage did not become "names" like the Beatles did, their music met a warm response from intellectual rockers. United States of America, a group on the Columbia label, even titled their second LP *Charles Ives' American Metaphysical Circus.* And Cage, with his interests in Zen Buddhism and the musical possibilities of electronic technology, struck many of the young people who had turned onto Eastern philosophy, Marshall McLuhan and Hermann Hesse's *Siddhartha,* as a kindred spirit.

And so, by the late 60s, a roster of role models existed for both art music composers and rockers who wanted to break through the proscriptive boundaries of their respective musical genres. What were now needed were vibrant forms for new music, so that explorations into new sounds, technologies, and performance techniques didn't wind up with either the tedious, disconnected works offered by older avant-garde serialists or the slapdash self-indulgences of psychedelic rock. At first, these forms were found in the exotic music of distant shores. In time, though, they were found much closer to home.

Discography

The Beatles	SERGEANT PEPPER'S LONELY HEART'S CLUB BAND	*Capitol/EMI SMAS-2653*
Velvet Underground	1969 VELVET UNDERGROUND LIVE	*Mercury SRM-2-7504*
Arnold Schoenberg	FIVE PIECES FOR ORCHESTRA: Op. 16; A SURVIVOR OF WARSAW: Op. 46	*Columbia M-35882*
Charles Ives	STEEPLES AND MOUNTAINS: CHROMATIMELODTUNE	*Nonesuch 71222*
Pierre Boulez	PLI SELON PLI	*Erato Num 75050*
John Cage	CONCERTO FOR PREPARED PIANO AND CHAMBER ORCHESTRA	*Nonesuch 71202*
Igor Stravinsky	THE RITE OF SPRING	*Columbia M-31520*

EAST MEETS WEST

It was 1965. Young people in the United States and Europe, growing up in material comfort, wondered if that was all there was. Eastern mysticism, with its goal to absorb the individual and all his troubles into the eternal godhead, seemed a way out of this malaise. In the 40s and 50s, small groups of bohemians had meditated and read the books of D.K. Suzuki that were written to introduce westerners to Zen. But the search for the All-In-One grew into a mass hunt in the 60s. Evangelistic groups like the Hari Krishna cult attracted thousands of devotees worldwide. The Maharishi Mahesh Yogi packaged Yogic meditation as a form easily learned by westerners—you pay your fee, you take the course, and you meditate to transcendence. Centers for Transcendental Meditation ("T.M.," as it was called) sprang up on college campuses, and in cities and small towns.

Along with this spiritual interest, people began to take notice of non-Western instrumentalists and dancers. For decades Ude Shankar had been touring the West with his Indian dance troupe, and he would often bring his nephew Ravi along. Ravi, in turn, was a highly accomplished sitar player, and toured with musicians Ulan Khan and his son Ali Akbar Khan. In 1965, Ravi Shankar met Beatle George Harrison at a party. "At that time," Shankar recounted in a recent radio interview, "I had never heard anything about the Beatles." Harrison was already interested in the sitar (a nineteen-stringed instrument that could handle a vast number of scales and scale systems) and wanted to learn to play it. He flew back to India with Shankar and studied with him for six weeks. And then, Shankar says, "It was like a sitar explosion all of a sudden. I became superstar (sic)." Soon the Beatles and the Rolling Stones were not the only rock groups using the sitar; the Doors had a sitar solo lasting twelve minutes in one of their songs. Raga-rock became one aspect of the psychedelic sound. Obviously, the rock format didn't allow for the complexity of ragas; the sitar and its scales were used merely as exotic sounds along with others being tried during that era. Shankar was a mature 46 at the time, and was quickly disillusioned with the West's interest in his culture when, under a two-year contract, producers tried to stick him

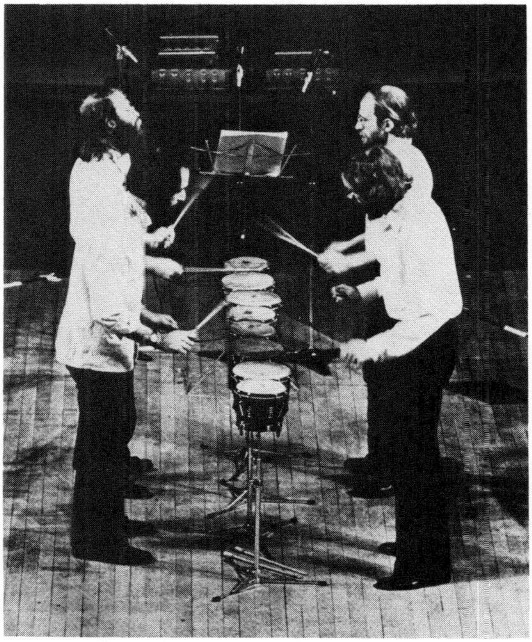

Courtesy of Ellen Jacobs Assoc.

Steve Reich—the composer of "Drumming," which these musicians are performing—was convinced that percussion could be the dominant voice in a piece.

David Redfern/Retna Ltd.

Ravi Shankar, India's premier sitarist, tutored George Harrison and started the 60s sitar explosion.

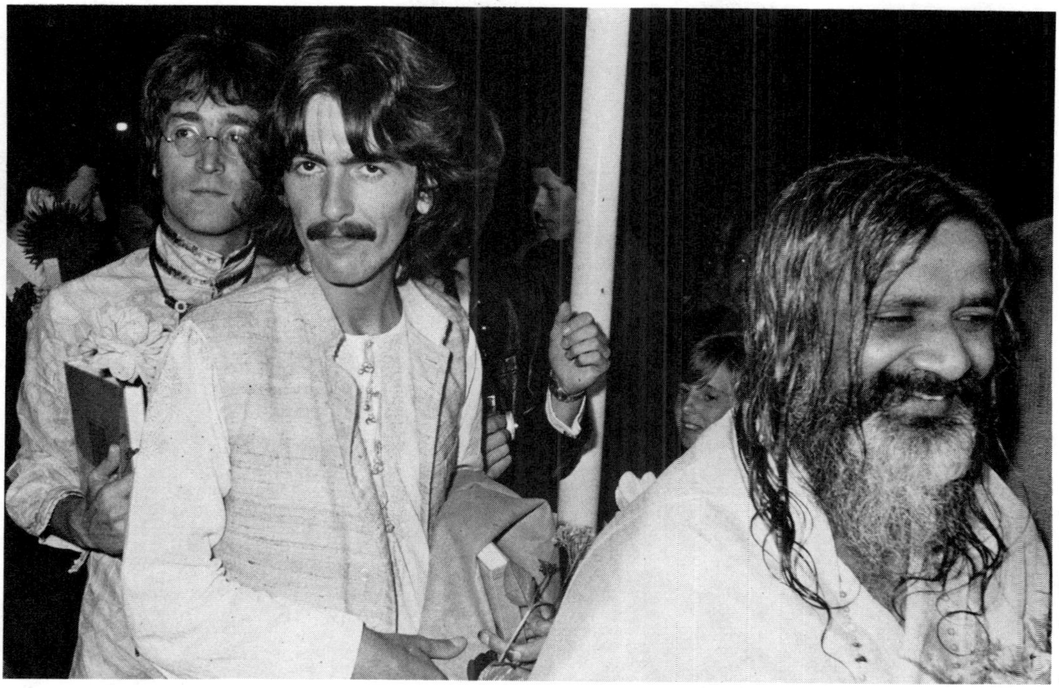

Camera Press/Photo Trends

Eastern mysticism, alluring if only half-understood, was a vital force in late 60s rock.

between hard-rock groups in stadium concerts. He also found the connection between the youth culture's interest in his culture and their interest in drugs disappointing. "LSD is Western Yoga," said Dr. Timothy Leary of *The Electric Koolaid Acid Test* fame. "The aim of all Eastern religion, like the aim of LSD, is basically to get high; that is, to expand your consciousness and find ecstacy and revelation within."

That same year—1965—composer Philip Glass, living and studying in Paris, was restless and bored. He had gone there to soak up the wisdom of esteemed French pianist and teacher Nadia Boulanger. Boulanger had tutored several generations of noted American musicians, among them Aaron Copeland and Virgil Thomson, now considered America's two grand old men of music. Perhaps Boulanger hoped twenty-eight-year-old Glass would follow in their footsteps; Glass, however, saw things differently.

He had studied music since he was eight years old: flute and piano and later, composition and harmony. Growing up in Baltimore, where his father owned a record store, Glass was exposed to a wide variety of music—from art music to jazz—as a boy. At the University of Chicago he majored in philosophy, but a career in music seemed in the cards for him, and in 1960, he enrolled at the Julliard School of Music in New York City. His study in Paris followed.

By his early twenties, Glass had already had several pieces of music published. All of these compositions, however, were in the dry, academic, serialist style that had come to characterize postwar American music. Today he disowns them.

While he was in Paris things started to change. Glass realized just how dissatisfied he was with his own music, and with the serial music that had been his model. It was 1967, he was nearly thirty, and very confused.

With a decisive nod of his head, Philip Glass cues his ensemble for a change to the next musical module.

Babette Mangolte

But then, a happy coincidence occurred, one which set Glass on a new path pursued by many of today's pop experimentalists. In Paris, the soundtrack to *Chappaqua,* a film by Conrad Brooks imbued with hippiedom's Eastern yearnings, was being put together. Its composer was Ravi Shankar. To be recorded as a soundtrack, Shankar's score first had to be transcribed into Western notation, and Glass got the job of transcribing it.

Glass' first encounter with classical Indian music proved to be a turning point. It was not just the sound of the sitar—so alluring to rock musicians like George Harrison—that fascinated Glass. Rather, he was drawn to the intricate structures—as opposed to rock's use of the surface sounds and scales of the sitar—of Indian music, especially the repeated rhythmic modules which were added onto or subtracted from one another to form longer or shorter units. These structures create a different sense of time. Unlike typical Western art music with its high points and low points, Indian music does not develop, or "go anywhere." Instead, it explores a single feeling at length, and stays at the same energy level throughout.

Before sitting down to write pieces inspired by Indian music, Glass explored other non-Western music including Moroccan and African music. He also made his first of several trips to Tibet and India in the mid-60s. By the time he returned to New York in 1967, he already had a clear idea of the music he wanted to compose.

Glass was not the only young and restless composer to be drawn to non-Western music during the mid-60s. Steve Reich was mad for the gripping, sensual rhythms of both jazz and Stravinsky's *The Rite of Spring* ever since he was a kid, and was naturally attracted to the even more complex polyrhythms of West African drumming, and hypnotic, rhythmic skeins of Balinese gamelan music. But he didn't really investigate either until 1963 (after he had been experimenting himself with rhythms using tape loops), when composer Gunther Schuller told him about a book called *Studies in African Music* by A.M. Jones. The book made a big impression on him. "I had heard African music—I knew they used drums—but it might as well have fallen from the moon. I had no idea what they were doing to produce that sound. And the book showed, basically, repeating patterns with the downbeat [the first beat of a measure] not coinciding, and basically what we would call twelve-meter—12/8—and of course a completely different way of putting together music than what we are used to. It immediately reminded me of what I was doing with the tape loops. It was as if I was seeing little mechanized Africans going around and around . . . and so what happened was—after having done *Piano Phase, Violin Phase,* and *Phase Patterns* that was actually drumming on the keyboards of electric organs—in 1970 I got a grant to go to Ghana—I could have stayed longer but I got malaria—and I have to say, really, I didn't learn anything I didn't know beforehand, but I got a kind of giant pat on the back which was saying something like, 'yes, percussion can be the dominant voice in the orchestra, yes, percussion is as exciting and perhaps richer in sound, than electronic instruments: go ahead.' " Reich got other green lights when he studied Balinese music during 1973 and 1974, and Yemenite and Iraqi Hebrew cantillation in the late 1970s. He found these similar to African music because of their interlocking, recurrent patterns and melodic cycles. Through these studies he was able to transform his tape-loop-derived phase music—in which short, taped rhythmic modules are repeated and overlapped and which don't exist in any culture—into music which was as rhythmically exciting, yet more suited to human performance, and eventually even playable by existing symphony orchestras.

Reich's experiments with rhythm were also inspired by Terry Riley and Riley's colleague, LaMonte Young. California-born Riley, a couple of years older than Reich and Glass, started out playing ragtime piano and jazz music, then began composing repetitive, somewhat improvisatory, Indian-related pieces in the mid-60s. The seminal *In C* of 1964 was built up from brief musical units that the various performers were free to play on almost any instrument they felt like playing—and free, too, to stop or repeat those units at will.

LaMonte Young had also been heavily involved in jazz before becoming interested in long, repetitive pieces that set a meditative, very Indian mood. It was natural that both Riley and Young became more directly involved with Indian music. Young began to study music with guru Pandit Pran Nath in 1970, to whom he found himself drawn "like iron filings to a magnet." Pandit gave him musical information, he says, "that had never even been hinted at in the history of Western classical music." Young brought Pandit to New York and, later, became his religious disciple. Now Young spends six hours daily studying Indian classical music, and the "subtle nuances of raga" influence his own compositions "by osmosis," as he recently told *Time* magazine. Terry Riley, too, began studying with Pandit Pran Nath after the latter's arrival in New York.

In fact, Glass', Reich's, Riley's, and Young's interest in non-Western music was nothing all that new for Western composers, at least in some respects. For example, during the mid-eighteenth century, Mozart and Gluck sprinkled musical orientalisms into several of their works, to create an air of exotic mystery. Later, in the late nineteenth century, some of Rimsky-Korsakov's music—most notably the ever-popular *Scheherezade*—is liberally perfumed with them. In all three cases, though, the music's structure was traditionally Western, with lulls, build-ups, climaxes, and subsidings. Musical orientalisms suffered a certain lack of understanding by Western composers. Like raga-rockers, they caught the sound of the East, but not the substance.

Claude Debussy was perhaps the first Western art music composer who grasped not just the superficial sound of non-Western music, but its deeper spiritual meaning. Debussy was introduced to Javanese music at the Paris World Exhibition in 1889. Writing in 1913, he recalled its profound effect on him. "There used to be—indeed, despite the troubles that civilization has brought, there still are—some wonderful peoples who learn music as easily as one learns to breathe," he wrote. "If one listens to it without being prejudiced by one's European ears, one will find a percussive charm that forces one to admit that our own music is not much more than a barbarous kind of noise more fit for a traveling circus."

Non-Western influences in Debussy's music are heard most clearly only in some of his smaller-scaled piano pieces. And yet, he set a precedent for such diverse composers as Carl Orff, John Cage, Harry Partch, Lou Harrison, and Olivier Messiaen. All these composers now draw on non-Western music while composing their own. Particularly inspiring were Indian, Indonesian, and African music with their bold rhythms, curious modal scales that sound neither happy nor sad, clear-cut melodies, hypnotic repetitions, and static, undramatic, almost impersonal qualities. These composers understood both the philosophical basis of non-Western music and its structures and sounds. Through that music, they found new ways of experiencing the world—ways tied to elemental forces and a sense of timelessness that has nothing to do with the "clock time" by which Westerners live out their lives. What's more, non-Western music, linked to religious or tribal rituals that still hold meaning for the people taking part in them, struck these composers as a means of pumping new life into Western art music, of making it more than just something to listen to at a concert on a night out. Indeed, they saw it as a means of transcending daily life, and entering a higher state of consciousness. Rather than provide mere entertainment, works like Cage's *Sonatas and Interludes for Prepared Piano,* Orff's *Catulli Carminae* and *Trionfi di Afrodite,* Messiaen's *Turangalila-Symphonie,* Harrison's *Three Pieces for Gamelan with Soloists,* and Partch's *Castor and Pollux* lift listeners up to ecstatic heights unattainable in daily life.

Rock, of course, had non-Western—specifically, African—music in its bones from the very start. It contains the vocals that are by turns incantatory and inarticulate, and the gyrations of its performers and audiences. After the 60s raga fad, groups like Mahavishnu Orchestra and Oregon developed the Indian vein of rock further. Other rock musicians absorbed African rhythms far more complex than those which were audible in early rock. So the links between rock and non-Western musics are not all that surprising. Wilfrid Mellers, in his book *Twilight of the Gods,* finds a great deal in common between the ritual music, from the "repetition, order, and rhythmic alteration inducing rapture and trance" to the distortion of pitch in both voice and instruments which is intensified by amplification. Showing the connection between cult possession rites and rock, Mellers quotes anthropologist Mary Douglas: "The more [the participant] is inarticulate, the more proof that [he] is unconscious and not in control of what is being imparted to him. Inarticulateness is taken as evidence of divine inspiration. So are 'dancing in the spirit'. . . and involuntary twitching and shuddering taken to be a sign of blessing."

Rhythms that lull or stir muscles and minds; simple, catchy melodies; overwhelming intensity to the point of loss of self by both performers and listeners—these qualities distinguish both rock *and* non-Western music. It is no wonder that the two blend so well. And now, with the interplay between world music, art music, and rock music finally being recognized, it makes sense that today's popular experimentalism resounds with non-Western influences.

But there are influences and there are influences. Some composers have looked to the East and written pieces that more or less copy the exotic sounds of the music. Lou Harrison is a prime example of this. Others, like Olivier Messiaen, use Eastern rhythms only as one element of music that is often extremely complex. Experimentalists like Terry Riley, Philip Glass and Steve Reich take neither of these approaches. Instead, these composers use Western instruments and harmonies and keep their music simple—more like the keyboard music of Cage, as well as the works of Partch and Orff.

But if the instruments they write for are Western, the effect of music by Reich, Riley, and Glass recalls that of non-Western music. Theirs is music that makes you want to get up and dance in movements of your own invention. Or, it soothes you into a calm, meditative state. Of course, the original Eastern music brought on ceremonial trances and dances. For example, ragas have a specific devotional purpose. Indeed, according to LaMonte Young, the most important duty in performing a classical Indian raga is to establish the spirit of the raga, each of which is related to a particular Hindu deity. *Raga Bupali,* for example, based on a special pentatonic scale, is associated with Shiva and the Himalayas. On the other hand, the Western counterparts are purely secular. When you listen to Steve Reich's *Music for Mallet Instruments, Voices, and Organ,* for instance, you don't focus on Gatucacha, or Arjuna, or any other denizens of the Balinese cosmology which the music that was inspiring Reich was invoking. You are more apt to let your thoughts go where they will: you think of taking a bath, walking in a parking lot by a beach, or of something you heard that bothered you; of how, if you view that remark from a new angle as suggested by a turn of phrase in the music, everything will be okay. . . . As you listen, your sense of time dwindles; your feet tap; your head nods; your body sways in time with the music. Your ears are seduced by the gentle female voices, the rippling marimba notes, the consoling, long-held tones of the electric organ. Your mind loses track of where the repetitions begin and end; each one sounds different. It isn't always 1-2-3-4, 1-2-3-4, but 1-2-*3*-4, *1*-2-3-4, *1*-2-*3*-4, changing over and over and over, and you close your eyes, and the music becomes a corridor down which you are gliding. A chime sounds, and in the corridor a velvet curtain rises, revealing a tableau: two tyrannosaurus rexes

David Redfern/Retna Ltd.

John McLaughlin, leading the Mahavishnu Orchestra, carried rock's Indian sound into the 70s.

with red, human thumbs, poised in front of a backdrop of palm trees and volcanos. Your thoughts float freely over the scene, the clouds in the vermillion sky on the backdrop actually move past slowly, so maybe it's not a backdrop after all. And then, subtly, the music shifts, and next to this scene appears another: A bare, stony stage cast in rainy light, a lone figure seated on it, with head in hands—slowly a tiny window on the back wall fills with pale yellow light, while the dinosaurs move their jaws as if they were speaking. The music holds. You watch both scenes, so different from one another, though as the music plays on it makes them seem somehow part of the same play. And then, another change: To the left of the dinosaurs and to the right of the stone room two more scenes appear. On the left is a baseball diamond, but with a catcher so huge that he blocks out most of the sunlit stadium beyond. And on the right is a scene in a modern bank, with people on line looking peeved and tellers moving behind a Plexiglas wall, laughing, counting out money, stamping receipts. The four scenes play simultaneously and, as the music continues, all assume an air of calm nobility that makes the bank boredom, the stone room isolation, the dinosaurs' soundless conversation and the hard-to-see ball game all right. It's as if all were exactly as they should be, nothing need be changed. . . . And two more new scenes materialize alongside the others: a Busby Berkley extravaganza of dancing penguins and flying storks as well as a control room with scientists,their backs to you, watching a rocket lift off on a TV monitor. And now the music is richly textured and flowing smoothly, as the next person heads for the next open teller, bankbook in hand, and the dinosaurs turn as the clouds congeal slowly into dinosaur shapes and the man in the stone room begins to eat a sandwich and the giant catcher steps aside to reveal a player sliding onto third base while the crowd in the bleachers stands up and cheers and the scientists keep watching the rocket lift off and the penguins skate on ice as silver as a mirror in patterns ever more intricate while the storks fly overhead, back and forth, each one carrying a bundle in its beak, and the music pursues its unhurried course. You are dazzled by this variety that, thanks to the music, is a unity even as each scene retains its difference from all the others. Yes, and now all the scenes are taking on the same golden radiance, then slowly starting to fade until they vanish, and all you can see is an endless field of wheat under a cloudless sky on a breezy day as the music holds, holds, holds. The whole experience confirms that, as composer Reich himself puts it, "Space is the place." For obviously, as Reich had been saying since 1969, "music should put all within listening range into a state of ecstasy."

Actually, *Music for Mallet Instruments, Voices and Organ,* written in 1973, several years after Reich had integrated Eastern musical forms into his own works, is one of the easier non-Western-related pieces to listen to and become enveloped by. The pieces Reich, Riley, and Glass wrote after their first encounters with Eastern music make more demands on the listener. Glass' Indian-influenced *Two Pages,* Reich's African-sounding *Phase Patterns,* and Riley's *In C* share a similar repetitiveness and purity, even though they sound completely different, with the Glass piece dark and throbbingly intense, the Reich piece all brilliant continual flares of light, and the Riley piece softer, like a murmuring stream.

At first, most listeners found these early works hard to take. All three of them are played at a high volume; repeat brief, simple, slightly varied, logically arranged musical patterns; stay in the same key and at the same tempo for as long as an hour and a half; and consist of as few as five notes, all of the same rhythmic value, played over and over again.

Indeed, composers of complicated serial works hated this music, which became known as minimalism, a term that, strangely but aptly, equated the music related to mystic and ecstatic religions with the sculptures and paintings of Judd, Lewitt, Marden, and Kelly—art that used simple geometrics in logically ordered series. Musicians and conductors wanted nothing to do with it either, and so Glass and Reich both had to form ensembles of their own. Glass' featured amplified female voices, keyboards, and woodwinds, and Reich's included accoustic percussion instruments, keyboards, and several female voices. In the end, though, all this hostility worked in their favor. For while both serial music and the equally complicated-sounding works of composers like Elliott Carter were played only in concert halls, Glass and Reich, relegated to pariah status, played everywhere else: art galleries, museums, lofts, and alternative music venues. What's more, in today's package-minded society, the fact that "The Philip Glass Ensemble" and "Steve Reich and Musicians" played *only* the works of their founders gave the music an instant visibility denied that of art composers like Carter, Milton Babbitt, and Arnold Schoenberg's lesser-known progeny, whose names vanish amidst the credits for concert programs they are only a part of. Thanks to this visibility, and of course to the music's tremendous appeal, Glass' and Reich's works came to be heard everywhere from Carnegie Hall to The Bottom Line nightclub to cities throughout Western Europe. Indeed, by the late 70s, composers of complicated music glared with envy, for Reich, Glass, and Riley had far larger audiences than they could ever hope for.

It should be noted that the success of these three composers had as much to do with the sort of music they were writing as it did with the audiences. By the mid 70s, Riley, Glass, and Reich had all changed their tunes. Their music became less austere. Riley's music—*Rainbow in Curved Air,* for instance—became lusher-sounding and more improvisational than the earlier *In C.* Glass' four-hour-long *Music in Twelve Parts* boasted short melodies that had a reassuringly familiar sound to them, evident despite the repetitions. By the end of the piece, equally (and intentionally) simple and familiar harmonic modulations cropped up, lending variety to the sameness. Reich's *Music for 18 Musicians* offered harmonic riches from its very first moments, memorable (if fragmentary) tunes, and sensual scoring for piano, marimba, voice, clarinet, violin, cello, xylophone, metallophone, and maracas.

But, though more accessible, this music was as non-Western as ever, and as challenging to Western listening habits. The musical patterns were formulaic, and levels of loudness and tempo stayed the same throughout a piece. There were more surprises, such as sudden harmonic shifts, but still no climaxes. The philosophic outlook underlying the music remained the same, too—an outlook Philip Glass summed up on the liner notes of *Music in Twelve Parts, Part 1 and 2:* "The music is placed outside the usual time-scale, substituting a non-narrative and extended time-sense in its place . . . When it becomes apparent that nothing 'happens' in the usual sense, but that, instead, the gradual accretion of musical material can and does serve as the basis of the listener's attention, then he can perhaps discover another mode of listening—one in which neither memory nor anticipation (the usual psychological devices of programmatic music, whether baroque, classical, romantic, or modern stic) have a place in sustaining the texture, quality or reality of the musical experience. It was hoped that one would be able to perceive the music as a dramatic structure, a pure medium of sound."

The recent works of Glass, Reich, and Riley are so richly textured and varied that, despite their inherent repetitions, they can no longer be termed minimalist. However, non-Western musical influences still abound. Reich's *Tehillim,* in which he sets four Hebrew psalms to eminently whistlable music inspired in part by Hebrew melodies, has a celebratory, quasi-religious aspect. Glass' *Dance No. 5,* with its asymmetrical, rapidly shifting, rhythmic patterns, extends his compositional techniques, though it stands as far outside the usual time-scale of Western music as his earlier works. On *Glassworks,* the composer's first LP for CBS Masterworks, Glass actually set time limits for himself similar to those that govern Western pop songs. Here, however, you get instrumentals that only last five or six minutes, but that, through repetition, try to change your sense of time just as non-Western music does. Another example is Riley's *Cadenza on the Night Plain,* a nearly hour-long work for a string quartet, that is a veritable parade of rhythmic patterns and brilliantly hued sounds.

But, perhaps the most striking change in this music has been its shift from trance-inducing evenness to a more explicit and varied emotionality. It is this shift that gives some of Steve Reich's latest works a feeling more like that of traditional Western art music, despite their non-Western repetitions. Reich himself is aware of this trend in his work. He notes that "there was, very obviously, a period in which I was very interested in non-Western music and I think that this was an incredibly fertile, healthy influence that has now become a permanent part of my vocabulary... however... looking back, older or recent Western music... has become exceedingly useful for me and I can see that continuing for some time."

And so we get a piece like Reich's *The Desert Music,* parts of which are not all that different from the music of more conservative American art-music composers such as Leonard Bernstein. Scored for a large orchestra and chorus, the work consists of William Carlos Williams poetry set to music. While the words are often inaudible in performance, after reading the poems on the program, it is hard to miss the messages Reich wants to convey: deep concern over the threat of nuclear holocaust, hope for the possibility of avoiding it, and the consolation music can provide in these dark times. Inevitably, such a weighty subject calls for music that expresses the web of feelings these issues arouse in all of us—optimism, fear, doubt, and relief—rather than ecstatic trance music. Accordingly, *The Desert Music* has a much less hypnotic, ritualistic quality than the messageless, consistently exalted *Music for 18 Musicians.* Its varied emotions come across loud and clear, and the piece has a hopeful, yet at the same time ambivalent mood. At present, Reich is at work on a piece for percussion ensemble. It will be interesting to see whether he returns to the emotionally neutral style of his music up until the mid-70s—a style that lets the listener bring his or her own emotions to the music—or whether he will develop along more traditional Western lines of musical thought.

Not all of today's non-Western-influenced music is as clearly structured as the works already discussed. Nor are they as intricately patterned or crisp sounding. So-called New Age composers, such as Deuter (a.k.a. Chaitanya Hari), Kitaro, Hans-Joachim Roedelius, and Harold Budd were, like Riley, Reich, and Glass, all inspired by Eastern music. However, they tend to play up its floating, less clear-cut, more improvisational qualities—which are derived from Indian classical music—at the expense of rhythm. The New Age composers furnish us with beds of slow-shifting sound, sweet, sad melody fragments, and pretty harmonies, with the occasional crashing wave, chirping cricket, and shrieking seagull. A little of this music goes a long way. Often it works best as a sonic background to meditate by. It is not incredibly intriguing musically, however, and can verge on the syrupy and banal.

On the other hand, composer Jon Hassell's music is more sophisticated. Hassell was drawn to Indian and African music not only for the structural models they offered, but because of the way they are linked to the rhythms of the natural world, and speak to both one's spiritual and sensual sides. In his own music, Hassell notes, he tries to express what he hears in non-Western music—"calmness, and a profound sense of what it's all about—meaning sex and life and death and all the things that come in between." Yet Hassell knows that such music will not fit easily into the wildly pluralistic, technological Western world. A captivating compromise between these two worlds, the music on such Hassell albums as *Possible Music* and *Magic Realism* exude what the composer calls "a sense of glamorous spirituality." Here, the melodies, drones, rhythms, structures, improvisations of classical Indian music, and the campy exoticisms of Hollywood film music of the 40s and 50s blend in surprising ways.

Like Glass and Reich, Hassell also brings a Western art-music background to his work. He received an M.A. in composition from the Eastman School of Music in Rochester, New York, and studied with Karlheinz Stockhausen in Cologne from 1965 to 1967. He started playing the trumpet when he was thirteen, modeling his style on Miles Davis' recordings like "Around the Corner," replete with wa-wa pedal. The moment when Western and non-Western music came together for Hassell occurred in Rome in 1973, where he was performing with LaMonte Young. "I was warming up with these jazz-derived patterns on the trumpet. Then Pandit Pran Nath started singing the same pattern that I was playing, only taking it places that I'd never heard before." At that point, Hassell decided he wanted to study with the Indian musician for he recognized the rich cultural crosscurrents that flowed through his music. The result was a "glamorous spirituality" that becomes more glamorous all the time, with upcoming projects that include the tentatively titled stage work *Shadow Play,* to be directed by American wunderkind Peter Sellars, set designed by the Japanese superstar architect Arata Isozaki, and costumes by fashion's trend-setting Issey Miyake. It is due to premiere in 1985.

David Hykes, who composes for and directs The Harmonic Choir, is a composer whose interest in non-Western music led him to write pieces that sound a lot like their non-Western models. The short, gentle, immensely soothing pieces of *Hearing Solar Winds* are based on a Mongolian vocal technique in which a singer produces two notes simultaneously. He or she holds one note, then slowly moves his or her tongue forward to make overtones above the note being sustained. The music does not sound at all Western, as Glass' and Reich's works manage to. Hykes himself sees his compositions as capable of leading people to an "inner silence" unobtainable in today's loud world. As music critic Gregory Sandow notes, Hykes' "music really is, as he says, spiritual, or even in some non-denominational sense, sacred."
The composers we have discussed so far are not rock musicians. While the drive and amplified sound of Glass' and Reich's earlier pieces have a rocklike quality, their music, as well as the music of the other composers mentioned, lacks the rock characteristics of both lyrics and a three-minute duration. Nor is their music meant to be danced to—though several choreographers have used it to accompany their own dance pieces. Rather, they may be seen as art music composers who have been inspired by non-Western music, and whose work is more accessible than the typical, complicated, late twentieth-century art music.

At the same time, though, some of the most exciting rock bands have started getting into non-Western music more deeply than did the sitarists and droners of the 1960s. Indeed, many of these bands have taken their cue from composers like Reich and Glass. Most successful of them is Talking Heads. Its original members—David Byrne, Chris Frantz, and Tina Weymouth—all studied at the Rhode Island School of Design in Providence. While they were there, the two men started a band called The Artistics—a name indicating the course they hoped their careers would take. In 1974, they moved to New York. By the next year, Talking Heads—the name taken from TV lingo for face shots on news and talk shows—was playing New York clubs like CBGB's and The Bottom Line, while Byrne worked at an ad agency, Frantz as a stock boy at a designer furniture shop, and Weymouth (who married Frantz in 1977) in Henri Bendel's chic shoe department.

Success came slowly, but fast enough for them all to quit their jobs in 1977. From that point on they played and recorded full-time in America and Europe. And by '77, Harvard grad Jerry Harrison had joined the band as second singer, keyboard player, and guitarist, and they had a record contract with Sire in the bag.

From the outset, Talking Heads was known as an "art"—or intellectual—band. Certainly its members had a very un-rock image, with their clean-cut appearance, plain clothes, and slightly weirded-out effect. Actually, Weymouth belongs to a socially prominent New York family and is an admiral's daughter, and Frantz is a general's son, and they betray a keen self-awareness not usually associated with rock stars. "When we started it was mostly in reaction to what was happening," drummer Frantz has explained. "We were anti-show biz, anti-arrogant, anti-glitter, and anti-over-professionalism."

It is not surprising, then, to find that even in their earliest efforts, Talking Heads mined musical veins previously untapped by mere rockers. As New York Times music critic John Rockwell noted in 1976, "This music is structured in the conventional verse-and-chorus patterns of

Talking Heads' music boasts African-inspired drumming, electric instrumentation, and intriguing lyrics.

the three-minute Top Forty tune. But the disjunctions between the sections are so sharp and stylized that they take on an abstractly formal interest." This concern with form, as well as the band's spare sound, stemmed as much from the influence of the works of Philip Glass and Steve Reich as it did from earlier rock like that of James Brown, whose endless, hypnotic funk repetitions come as close as you can get to African and minimalist music.

Their interest in formal structure and in black American funk led Talking Heads to explore the highly structured, rhythmically precise but complex tribal music of Africa, as well as contemporary African pop of stars like Fela and King Sunny Adé. They were further encouraged

Lisa Haun/Retna Ltd

in this direction by rock musician Brian Eno, who produced Talking Heads' second album, and was himself fascinated by tribal music.

The African influence first became apparent with "I Zimbra," the opening cut on Talking Heads' third album, *Fear of Music,* another Eno production. The words, based on poetry by the 20s German dadaist Hugo Ball, were nonsense syllables that recalled the anti-art gestures some disaffected German poets made just after World War I. But the driving beat was African enough to give the song the sound of a tribal chant.

That chantlike quality is even more evident in the songs on *Remain in Light,* Talking Heads' fourth album, as are the thrillingly kinetic, danceable rhythms and the mesmerizing, repetitious melodies that grow out of them. Here the textures become denser as the band's original quartet grew to include members from black bands such as Labelle, Ashford & Simpson, and Parliament-Funkadelic.

For the shy, gangly, "wacko" Byrne, African music offered a means of making music that was "a way out of being lumped as the loony—rock's answer to 'Psycho's' Tony Perkins." But there is more to it than that, as Byrne himself notes. "In the African tradition, we had to learn when *not* to play, and that goes against a rock musician's capitalistic way of thinking, which is to get as much as you can for yourself. In sacrificing our egos for mutual cooperation, we get something—dare I say it?—more spiritual." Not only more spiritual—the word applies to music by Riley, Reich, Glass, Hassell, and Hykes as well—but more boldly and showily cross-cultural, too. It is music that is in a way totally in synch with an era when, thanks to electronics and rapid modes of transportation, the world is becoming the Global Village people called it in the 60s, although not an especially cute or cozy one.

Later, Talking Heads members took on solo projects as a relief from intergroup tensions, including Frantz's and Weymouth's *Tom Tom Club* (which featured their hit "Genius of Love") and *Close to the Bone;* Harrison's *The Red and the Black;* Byrne and Eno's collaboration *My Life in the Bush of Ghosts;* and Byrne's *Songs from the Broadway Production of The Catherine Wheel.* All these continued to explore African and funk polyrhythms, though with varying degrees of commercial success. In *Speaking in Tongues,* Talking Heads' fifth album (in which the band for the most part, shrinks back down to its four original members), the African influences are as evident as ever. Now that Brian Eno is no longer working with the band, though, the sound is again more spare and dry.

Despite its links with more art-music-oriented pop experimenters, the way in which Talking Heads takes on non-Western (specifically, African) music is in many ways quite different from the methods of, say, Steve Reich, whose *Drumming* and *Music for 18 Musicians* both bear certain African traits. To begin with, Talking Heads' music consists not of compositions, but of songs, although those songs can stray from the usual three-minute rock format. Secondly, Talking Heads' songs are meant to be danced to in clubs, unlike Reich's music, for instance, which is meant to be listened to by a seated audience. Thirdly, Talking Heads' songs have lyrics—verbal fragments that express feelings of dislocation, paranoia, alienation, or ironic, weary affirmation. The emotionality of the lyrics (which are written after the music) causes the music's African flavor to have not a spiritual tang but an undertaste of emotional obsession or giddy confusion. Still, it is this emotional directness that in part makes Talking Heads' music more accessible than music by Glass or Reich.

With their astonishing originality, it was inevitable that Talking Heads would inspire other rock bands to attempt excursions along non-Western paths. Some of the most interesting of these include Depeche Mode, the British synthesizer band that, in their song "Are People People?," creates a strange, jerky yet persistent chant against a background of industrial noises.

XTC's song "It's Nearly Africa" on their *English Settlement* album is less synthetic sounding, but also cooler and more straightforward in its use of African percussion instruments. A third British group, Bronski Beat, offers "Infatuation," a seductive instrumental that features rather simple but compelling African drumming. Indian music seems to hold less allure for rock musicians—certainly less than it did in the 60s. Indeed, when a group like Monsoon tries to fuse Indian classical and Western rock music, the result is like a parody of Indian-inspired Beatles' songs of the 60s.

Overall, rock, as is only natural considering its origins, seems much more compatible with African music nowadays. Englishman Malcolm McLaren, former manager of the Sex Pistols, was convinced this when he was in Paris, the home of many African musicians, looking for porno films. He brought back a batch of tapes (African, not porno) and encouraged a young punk rocker, Adam Ant, to use the roiling rhythms in his new band, Adam and the Ants. With Adam dumped from the band, Boy George became the lead singer for a while before Boy formed his own group, Culture Club, and McLaren found a new lead—fourteen-year-old Burmese beauty Annabella Lu Win—in a laundromat. The group then became known as Bow Wow Wow and had a hit in 1981 with the heavily African *See Jungle! See Jungle!* album on the Warner Brothers label.

Non-Western influences are omnipresent in pop experimentalism today. Still, not everyone agrees that those influences bode well for the West. Juliette Alvin, in her book *Music Therapy,* warns that "when rhythmical music repeats itself endlessly. . . there is no limit to its effects on primitive instincts . . . The frenzy of tribal or witches' dances, of bacchic orgies, was produced by music made of endless repetitive and conflicting rhythms." The late British composer-theorist Cornelius Cardew, in his book *Stockhausen Serves Imperialism,* condemned the mysticism of non-Western inspired music as "a tool for the suppression of the masses." Wim Mertens, in *American Minimal Music,* calls the pleasures such music gives "pseudo-satisfaction," adding that it "will probably serve to strengthen the historical impasse for the worse." Cardew and Mertens both feel that music in which the primary purpose is to produce ecstasy in listeners only stops those listeners from seeing what their lives are really like socially, politically, economically, psychologically, and maybe even spiritually, despite the music's supposedly spiritual aspirations. In light of this criticism, it is interesting to note the sort of work Glass and Reich, for example, are involved in at present, some of which deals very specifically with—and asks audiences to open their eyes still wider to—the real dangers brewing in the present world political struggle.

New directions notwithstanding, many people enjoy the non-Western-inspired music of pop experimentalists, whether it be the uplifting rhythms of Talking Heads or the trancelike 70s pieces of Reich and Glass. And, asks French critic Jean-Francois Lyotard, why *shouldn't* they enjoy it? Forget about what life is really like, says Lyotard in this music's defense. "In the age of the rising libido, being right is not important, laughing and dancing is what matters." Others see the music's appeal in less hedonistic terms. Recently William Rubin, curator of New York's Museum of Modern Art, offered an insight into the appeal non-Western art holds for people today. "There is a whole world of experience in tribal art that is just not dealt with in Western art before the twentieth century, " Rubin remarks. "We are getting back to certain roots, not just artistically, but of our own humanity and psychology." The same might be said about non-Western music. As discussed, non-Western music expresses religious outlooks that soothe listeners by telling them that, despite all evidence, the world is well-ordered and/or an illusion. If one chooses to see that as getting back to roots, that's fine. Certainly it is the sort of return that much of today's pop experimentalism encourages. What's more, the relief it offers is a balm against the way the world is today. Of course, it does not express the religious solidarity that makes ceremonial gamelan music so profoundly meaningful to the Balinese. But then, music by Philip Glass, Steve Reich, Terry Riley, Jon Hassell, Harold Budd, David Hykes, Talking Heads, and others can provide mystical experiences all by themselves. Given that fact—and the less palatable facts of life as it is today, at once mundane and terrifying—it is no wonder that this powerfully seductive music captivates us.

Discography

The Beatles	REVOLVER	*Capitol/EMI SW 2576*
Mahavishnu Orchestra	VISIONS OF THE EMERALD BEYOND	*Columbia PC33411*
Olivier Messiaen	TURANGALÎLA SYMPHONIE	*RCA Victor LSC-7051*
Philip Glass	MUSIC IN TWELVE PARTS: Parts 1 & 2	*Virgin Records Ltd. CA2010*
Steve Reich	DRUMMING; MUSIC FOR MALLET INSTRUMENTS, VOICES, AND ORGAN; SIX PIANOS	*Deutsche Grammophon 2740 106*
Steve Reich	MUSIC FOR 18 MUSICIANS	*ECM-1-1129*
Terry Riley	IN C	*Columbia Masterworks MS 7178*
Jon Hassell	FOURTH WORLD VOL. I: Possible Musics	*Editions EG EGS 107*
David Hykes with the Harmonic Choir	HEARING SOLAR WINDS	*Ocora 558 607*
Talking Heads	REMAIN IN LIGHT	*Sire Records SRK 6095*
Talking Heads	SPEAKING IN TONGUES	*Sire Records 23883-1*
James Brown	AIN'T THAT A GROOVE (1966-69)	*Polydor 422-821231-1*

NEW SOUNDS 2

On a deserted downtown New York street, a young man with the suit, stature, and eyeglasses of an underground Clark Kent is hitting everything in sight with drumsticks, keeping a rock rhythm. He tries out metal storefronts, telephone booths, and the sidewalk itself. And what do you know—all these items, when struck, produce vibrations, each with a sound of its own. No, this is not the type of guy who drums on mailboxes, his hair slicked down with shoe polish, his sanity gravely in doubt. No, that guy has found his instrument, his search is over. David Van Teighem, our subject, is still searching, still experimenting, as he drums out of sight down the street in a videotape by John Sanborn called *Ear to the Ground.* In another video, Van Teighem tries out the sonic properties of a playground in Tokyo. In a series of performances entitled *A Man and His Toys,* Van Teighem has hit everything from beach balls to Tupperware, toy pianos to thimbles, TV sets to automobile fanbelt pulleys, pipes of all kinds, and puppets. Other things don't have to be hit: toy monkey drummers and robots are wound up, explosives are set off, cap pistols are shot, and Alka-Seltzer is plopped. All this is done with a sense of rhythm and smooth body movement that expresses more than just noise—it says "music."

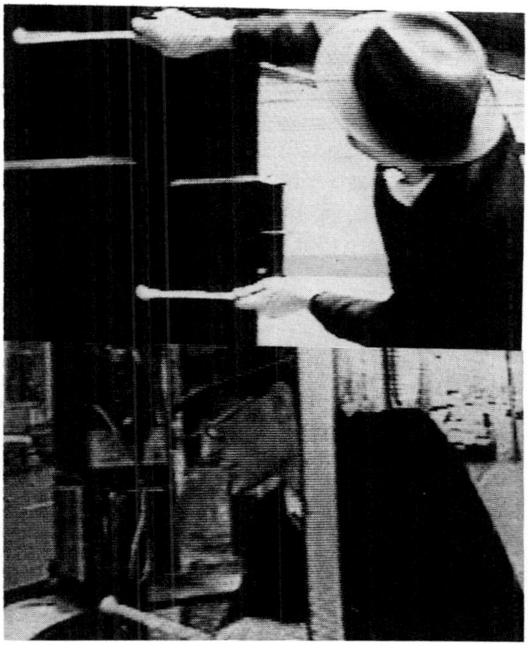

A & B—Robin Holland

In the video *Ear to the Ground,* David Van Teighem turns Manhattan into one gigantic musical instrument.

Ever since a tree fell in the forest and there was an ear to enjoy it, the search for new sounds has been an integral part of the human activity known as music-making. One can only speculate about the smiles on the faces of early humans when they smacked their clubs together just for the pleasure of hearing the sound, or when they listened to the variety of howls they could produce around a campfire.

By 2800 B.C., there is written evidence that the Chinese were already organizing sounds into the system of pitch relationships we call scales. Chu T'sai Yu, a sixteenth-century Chinese historian, says that the formulas for the five-note scale were worked out in China by 2700 B.C. In the West, in the fifth and sixth centuries B.C., the Greek philosopher Pythagoras worked out a system of ratios that associated string length and the number of vibrations per second. He called these ratios "the harmony of the spheres," and had virtually constructed the approximate twelve-note series that we use today. Modes were formed from this system by taking the basic diatonic scale—or the white keys on the modern piano starting with D, E, F, or G and going up. These modes formed the material of medieval church music. Each mode has a very specific sound and mood, almost like a tune. Modes can be used over one octave only and are very inflexible. But when sharps and flats are added, scales are created that can be used over many octaves and can create complex harmonies.

By the eighteenth century, when Bach wrote *The Well-Tempered Clavier,* scales had been adjusted, or "tempered," so that each major scale sounded almost exactly the same as any other (except that they were, of course, in different pitch ranges) so that you can move from one key to another on a piano without retuning it.

The resulting note system, normally used over a range of about seven octaves, provides an amazing number of possibilities for music: almost all Western music—from Bach to Culture Club—and much non-Western music uses it. It can be structured in many ways, from the sonata form to serialism to twelve-bar blues. It allows unlimited harmonies when tones are layered over each other. It can be made to express the full range of human emotions. The only problem is that, in the West, it is often believed that only sounds within this system, played on the instruments that developed along with it, were musical. Everything else was labeled "noise."

But there have always been visionaries who saw other possibilities. Francis Bacon, describing a utopia in his 1624 work *New Atlantis,* wrote: "We have harmonies which you have not, of quarter-sounds, and lesser slides of sounds [i.e. microtones]. Divers[e] instruments of music likewise to you unknown, some sweeter than any you have; together with bells and rings that are dainty and sweet. We represent small sounds as great and deep; likewise great sounds extenuate and sharp; we make divers[e] tremblings and warblings of sounds which in their original are entire."

By the mid-nineteenth century, mainstream composers, wishing to make their music richer and more varied, refused to limit themselves to existing musical instruments. Instead, they began to use sounds that reproduced the world outside the concert hall. At first, their romantic love of nature, combined with a desire to excite their audiences, spurred them on. For example, in his opera *Il Trovatore,* Verdi lent a realistic air to the gypsy camp setting in Act Two by scoring the famous "Anvil Chorus" for real anvils, as well as conventional instruments. Tchaikovsky used tubular bells and a cannon to heighten the drama of his *1812 Overture.* The cowbells Mahler included in his Sixth Symphony evoke the countryside, while the exotic gong chimes Puccini used in *Madame Butterfly* and *Turandot* enhance the Japanese flavor of those two operas. At the same time, new instruments were invented to improve upon similar sounding ones: the oboe-like heckelphone, for example, as well as the double-reeded sarrusophone and the organ-like harmonium. The most well-known of these new instruments was the saxophone, invented in Paris, in 1840, by Adolphe Sax. His intention was to create a brass, reed, and woodwind instrument with an immense amount of sonic versatility to be an all-around instrument for horse-mounted military bands.

In music of the early twentieth century, unusual and unexpected sounds were heard more and more often, to the point that sonic "special effects" sometimes became a piece's most noticeable feature. Or, an array of exotic and/or newly invented instruments simply tinged a moment in a piece. For instance, Igor Stravinsky set the tambourines rattling to heighten the barbarity of the "Evocation of the Ancestors" in *The Rite of Spring,* and Schoenberg used the guitar to lend a commedia dell'arte twist to *Pierrot Lunaire.*

Other composers continued to evoke the extra-musical world by using non-musical instruments in their works. As might be expected, the new sounds of the outside world that were being imitated became less pastoral as composers broke out of their romantic reveries and woke up in the middle of the Industrial Revolution. Georges Antheil included a car horn and buzz saw in his *Ballet Mécanique,* and Erik Satie incorporated a typewriter into *Parade.* The Futurists, a movement of poets, painters, and musicians in Italy in the 1910s and 1920s, were even more extreme. "Life in ancient times was silent," wrote Futurist Luigi Russollo, in a 1913 manifesto. "In the nineteenth century, with the invention of machines, noise was born." Instead of an orchestra composed of the usual strings, woodwinds, brass, etc., Russollo thought the modern orchestra should consist of six groups of noisemakers that would reproduce the mechanical world, accompanied by screams, animal voices, and snoring.

It wasn't until the mid-20s, though, with the French-American composer Edgard Varèse, that large, undiluted dollops of noise became accepted as music. Varèse sought to "liberate" sound, as he put it. In 1894, at the age of 11, he wrote an opera, but he then went on to study science and math at the University of Turin—his parents having encouraged him to become an engineer. But, instead, Varèse used his scientific studies as a way to find his own angle on music composition. Influenced by a scientist named Heimholz who had done an extensive study on sirens, Varèse envisioned a music made up of "beautiful parabolic and hyperbolic curves." After studying conventional composition at the Paris Conservatory, Varèse emigrated to the United States. In the 20s, he formed the International Composers Guild, an organization dedicated to performing new music, and with this supportive resource was able to present not only Schoenberg and Webern, but his own new sound pieces as well. *Hyperprism*, in 1923, used conventional wind instruments, and a wide variety of percussion instruments in discordant ways. The piece sounded like "a catastrophe in a boiler factory," according to a *New York Times* critic. Throughout the 20s, Varèse continued to use conventional instruments to construct unheard of sonorities, but soon he found them limiting.

In 1933, he composed *Ionisation,* a piece scored for 33 percussion instruments, including a piano on which tone clusters were pounded out. The emphasis of *Ionisation* is in the contrast of sonic colors or timbre—the quality of sound that makes a violin different from a flute, for example, even though both are playing the same note. To create the widest variety of these colors, Varèse designed special wood and metal objects for the piece. Critic Paul Rosenfeld, in his enthusiastic reaction to *Ionisation,* anticipated a growing interest in everyday noises as music: "The streets are full of jangly echoes. The taxi squeaking to a halt at the crossroads recalls a theme. Timbres and motives are sounded by police whistles, bark and moan of motor horns and fire sirens, mooing of great sea-cows steering through harbor and river, chatter of drills, in the garishly lit fifty-foot excavations. . . . A thousand insignificant sensations have suddenly become interesting, full of character and meaning." Noise had become music.

John Cage was a frontrunner in the development and experimentation of noise pieces after World War II, with prepared pianos and the like. Others, both in America and Europe, carried on in this direction. American Harry Partch built his own instruments with glass bottles and hubcaps, and even devised a tuning system consisting of tiny microtones to broaden the possibilities of his tunable instruments. Europeans like Luciano Beric, Karlheinz Stockhausen, Krysztof Penderecki, and György Ligeti usually did not invent new instruments. Instead, they instructed performers to play them in odd ways to produce surprising new sounds.

In the cases of Cage and Partch, the result was music that could be riveting, not so much because of the new sounds, but because of the strong, hypnotic rhythms of pieces like Cage's

Remy Charlip

The interior of John Cage's piano, specially "prepared" with household objects.

Sonatas and Interludes For Prepared Piano and Partch's *Daphne of the Dunes.* On the other hand, the European music, with its lack of melody, rhythm, and tonal harmony, was sometimes tedious and obscure once the dazzling novelty of these new sounds wore off. However, composers like American George Crumb based works of music around bizarre, colorful texts to which these equally outlandish sounds related, and succeeded—at least for a short time—in capturing a sizable audience.

The concerts where these new sonic possibilities—pieces by Varèse, Cage, Stockhausen, Berio, and others—were first revealed were high-culture affairs. The dead seriousness of it all discouraged listeners from tagging the sounds with their most obvious emotional labels, "funny" for the burps coming out of the bassoon, "irritating" for the screetches from the violin, "ghoulish" for the keening clarinet. The composer of such a piece of music clearly meant these sounds to be, not just sonic illustrations, but only one aspect of a dense interplay of counterpoints and harmonies. These "sound-colorist" concerts often had a decidedly mystical and ritualistic air, which *N.Y. Times* critic John Rockwell—in a discussion of George Crumb—described as "earnest academics wearing party masks and parading about solemnly while whacking percussion."

The mystical mood of sonic color music has certain parallels with the minimalism of the late 60s and early 70s. Audiences spaced out on the long-held tones of LaMonte Young and his followers, and acoustic researchers such as the Sonic Arts Union founded by Robert Ashley and Alvin Lucier, amplified Lucier's brain waves, and called it music. Indeed, hi-fi amplification opened up a host of possibilities for sound devotees, and to this day, in lofts and art galleries around the world, people are closely listening to everything from thin glass tubes stroked with a bow to water plinking into a galvanized steel washbasin.

While new sounds may have seemed like daring novelties in art music, they have always been the stock in trade of rock 'n' roll. A rock group trying to make it, finds original sound texture is as important, if not more important, than catchy tunes or stage theatrics. The greatest contribution to the characteristic sound of all rock was, of course, the invention of the instrument that joins an electric guitar, an amplifier, and the local utilities company. In the 30s and 40s, such innovators as Leo Fender and Les Paul experimented with the best placement of a pickup in a solid-body guitar (the traditional hollow-body was discarded early because of feedback problems). Jazz artist Charlie Christian and bluesman T-Bone Walker pioneered the single-note (as opposed to chord), hornlike lines that could now be played over a band with the electric guitar. The most popular ensemble for this instrument is the guitar band, as formatted by Buddy Holly and the Crickets in the early 50s. Two electric guitars—one lead and one rhythm—are accompanied by drums and bass—the role of the bass growing increasingly important. In the 60s, American garage bands and surf-music bands, and British-invasion bands made this the standard format for pop music. Even in the 80s, when total synthesizer bands are becoming more and more popular, the word rock still conjures up the image of three boys up front with their axes slung low, the drummer a wild blurr in the background, and an occasional keyboard, sax, or horn section somewhere on the edge of the TV screen.

Letting it all hang out, rock guitarists were driven to produce stranger and stranger noises from their new instruments. From the beginning, the "dirty" sound of an electric rock guitar differentiated it from its more refined jazz counterpart. This urge to "mess up" instrumental sounds might also come from the roots of rock: the rural black tradition of blues and the African vocal and instrumental tradition from which that, in turn, descended. John Storm Roberts, in his ground-breaking work *Black Music of Two Worlds*, points out that many African instruments had bits of extra material attached to them to add buzzing and rattling, and these extra-musical noises were often retained in the music of their descendents in the New World. Whatever the origin, the emotional frenzy considered typical to rock performers made them do worse and worse things to their instruments. Little Richard stamped on his keyboard. Bo Diddley played guitar with his teeth. Link Wray, the progenitor of the 50s hit "Rumble," who was "playin' rock 'n' roll before there was rock 'n' roll," as he explains, was self-taught "except for a black guy named Hambone" in a small town in North Carolina. Wray explains his sonic innovations: "I started searchin' for music sounds, you know, 'cause, I mean, I played jazz hot licks and I got bored with all them sophisticated hot licks and chords. . . . So I was lookin' for sounds, before there was any boxes [sound-modification gizmos]. I made my own wa-wa pedal from a pipe attached to an . . . outdoor driver, you know, a horn, the driver from that . . . I took a hose from that to my mouth, you know, and it come through the amplifier with my mouth, wuh-wuh-wuh, like that. . . . And fuzz—I stuck pencils . . . in my amplifier. And then I had a big speaker down there, and the tweeters, I used to stick holes in 'em . . . and then I used to use two amplifiers against each other to get the compressed sounds." He was clearly a man after Varèse's heart.

On the whole, though, early rock 'n' rollers did little to add to the sonic possibilities of their guitars. Through the early 60s, the electric guitar sound was the one we now associate with the surf and garage bands—the twangy, metallic sound of a Fender piped directly into an amplifier, with the amp's built-in echo and tremolo effects the only modifications. The mid-60s British bands began to be innovative again, using fuzz-tones (like the sound of the lead in the Rolling Stones' "Satisfaction"), possibly an attempt to reproduce the distortion of early blues recordings. And the post-*Sergeant Pepper* era was riddled with discordant noises and Indian modes in the rock bag of tricks.

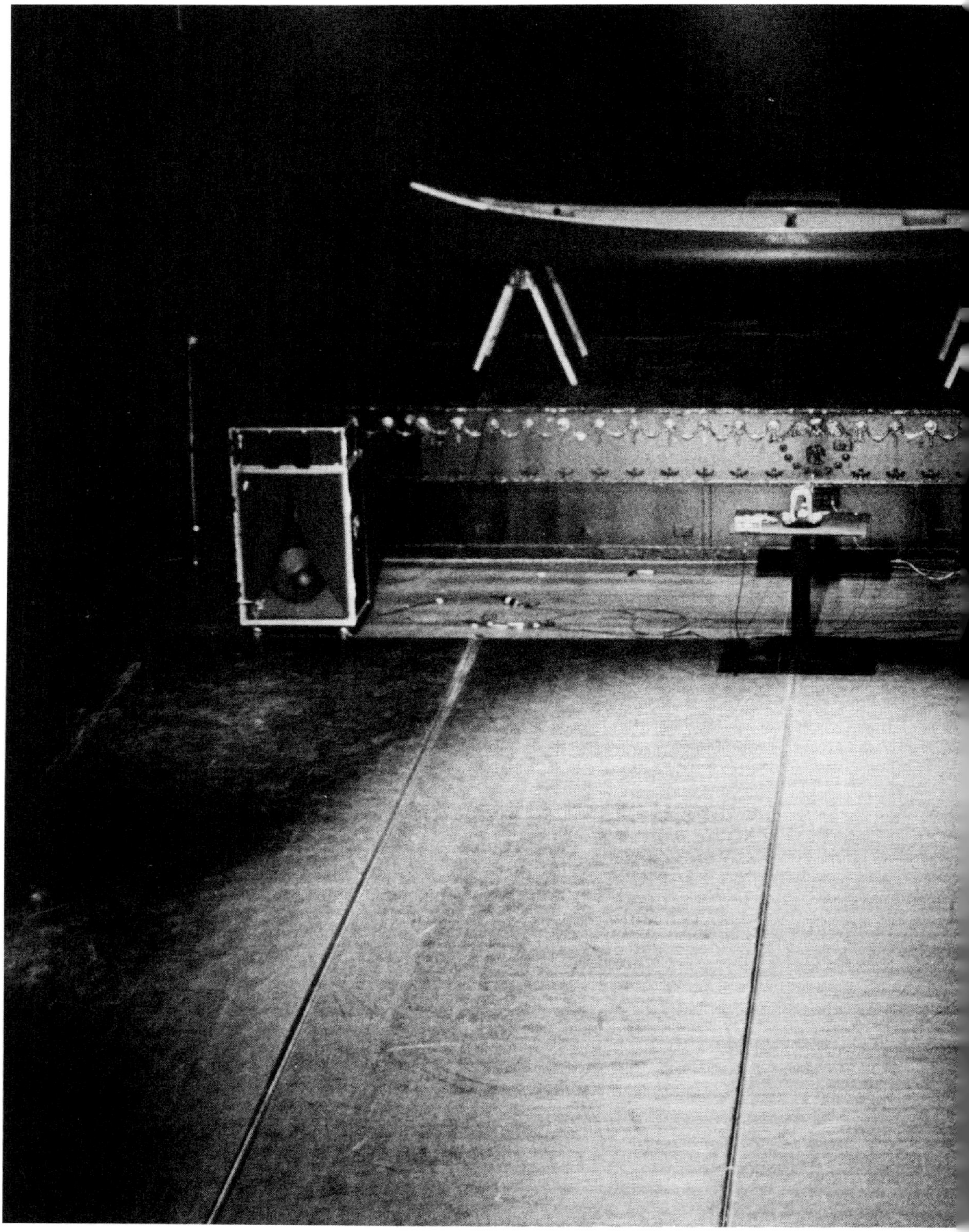

Alvin Lucier's studies in acoustical processes lead somewhere between science, mysticism, and dada.

Babette Mangolte

Keri Pickett

Known for his improvisational systems, John Zorn frequently solos duck calls blown through water.

In that post-*Sergeant Pepper* era David Van Teighem was in high school drumming with a rock band and they "just began getting weird." They played in the high school gym, "extending improvisation beyond notes," sometimes producing no sound at all while continuing to move about on the stage in a curious fashion. Van Tieghem says his penchant for weirdness was encouraged when he heard Frank Zappa and the Mothers of Invention in *Hot Rats* and *Burnt Weenie Sandwich,* which used "a lot more timbres and sounds than anyone else in rock at the time."

Van Teighem had begun his own search for new sounds as a four-year-old in New Jersey, hitting pots and pans on the kitchen floor. He'd practiced rock drumming since the age of twelve, playing along with records. But listening to the records his father, who worked with Contempo records, brought home, featuring such unusual treats as electronic music by Morton Subotnick, made him realize that there were greater sonic possibilities. The music of Varèse confirmed that there was immense freedom with percussion. One day, Van Tieghem heard an ad on a rock station for Steve Reich's *Music for 18 Musicians.* He went to the concert and was entranced. "I was amazed that a very serene feeling could be created in percussion and that it could still have an effect in the gut, with a lot more effects floating on top." As a student in the Manhattan School of Music, Van Teighem had an opportunity to audition for the Reich ensemble, was accepted, and soon became a highly sought-after percussionist, open to experimentation and collaboration. Now, he has worked with Charlotte Moorman (a Cage collaborator best known for her topless cellist performances), Peter Gordon and the Love of Life Orchestra, David Byrne and Brian Eno, Laurie Anderson, Robert Ashley, and a good many others.

When he thought about doing his own music, Van Tieghem knew he wanted to work with new sounds—and movement in performance—as related to percussion. But he didn't want to create either the staid atmosphere of the post-war sound colorists, or the mayhem of a rock concert. "I wanted it to be fun and at the same time serious about the sound." He visited junk shops, toy stores, flea markets, and "even pilfered a few ashtrays from restaurants" looking for new instruments. And, even though he uses these objects in unexpected ways, they retain their identities. With each performance, he is, in a sense, recreating his discovery of that object as a new sound source.

Back in the late 60s, The Yardbirds—at times including of Jimmy Page, Eric Clapton, and Jeff Beck—did the most of any rock group to create a guitar sound that became typical of "heavy" or "hard" rock, which lives on as heavy metal and punk. Beck ran his guitar through a Marshall amp that was turned up or "overdriven" to the point of distortion. Soon, a "box" —electronic gizmo—could produce it. Other boxes made wa-wa effects, echoes, reverberations, and sustain-and-decay effects. By 1968, Cream, the Kinks, the Who, and the Rolling Stones were all creating walls of distorted sounds. "There was the sound of mountains crashing in this holocaust of decibels," Norman Mailer wrote in 1968 after hearing a heavy-rock group called MC5. "Hearts bursting, literally bursting, as if this were the sound of death by explosion within . . . as insane and scalding as waves of lava . . . flushing through the urn of all acquired culture and sending . . . the brain like a foundered carcass smashing down the rapids, revolving through a whirl of demons, pool of uproar, discords vibrating, electric crescendo screaming as if at the electro-mechanical climax of the age."

Jimi Hendrix was the virtuoso of this distorted guitar sound, with his mountain range of overdriven amps skillfully recreating the firebombing of Dresden over the heads of the audience. "He would describe the sound he wanted in colors," says Hendrix's custom "box" maker Jack Kramer, "and sometimes it might be spatial and might include everything under the sun." Sometimes, though, Hendrix would be more literal, like when he was obsessed to hear what an underwater guitar would sound like. "He said," Kramer relates, " 'I really want to hear the sound of this thing underwater.' And I said okay . . . I went to a local radio shop and bought a couple of Styrofoam speakers . . . and I got a bucket of water, stuck the speakers into the water with the wires on, and cranked up the volume . . . It sounded awful."

The fuzz-distortion sound became pedestrian with the heavy-metal groups that kept it stagnated throughout the 70s and 80s and became the nightmare heroes of twelve-to-fifteen-year-old American boys. But the Velvet Underground and its successor, the New York Dolls, with noisy drones and straight-ahead buzz-saw guitarists, pushed the sound to places where it could develop more, into the sleazy big-city rock clubs such as CBGB's in New York, where groups like the Ramones reduced it to its real basics. *Cretin Rock,* the Ramones' first album, could not be called three-chord rock—there was only about one chord being played—but mainly it was lots of loud, high-energy noise. Whether or not the Ramones' 1976 tour caused it, this power noise exploded into punk in Britain, with thousands of safety-pinned kids trying with all their might to blow their amps. The Sex Pistols—a group produced by Malcolm McLaren and designed to outrage—were soon followed by the likes of the Slits, the Damned, the Clash, the Buzzcocks, and the Vibrators. As punk fragmented into the diversity

In the post-Varèse era, sound experimentation is widespread: here is British housewife, Linda Grant.

Syndication International/Photo Trends

Joseph Sia/Retna Ltd.

Jimi Hendrix crouches ecstatically between huge speakers and a battery of sound modification boxes.

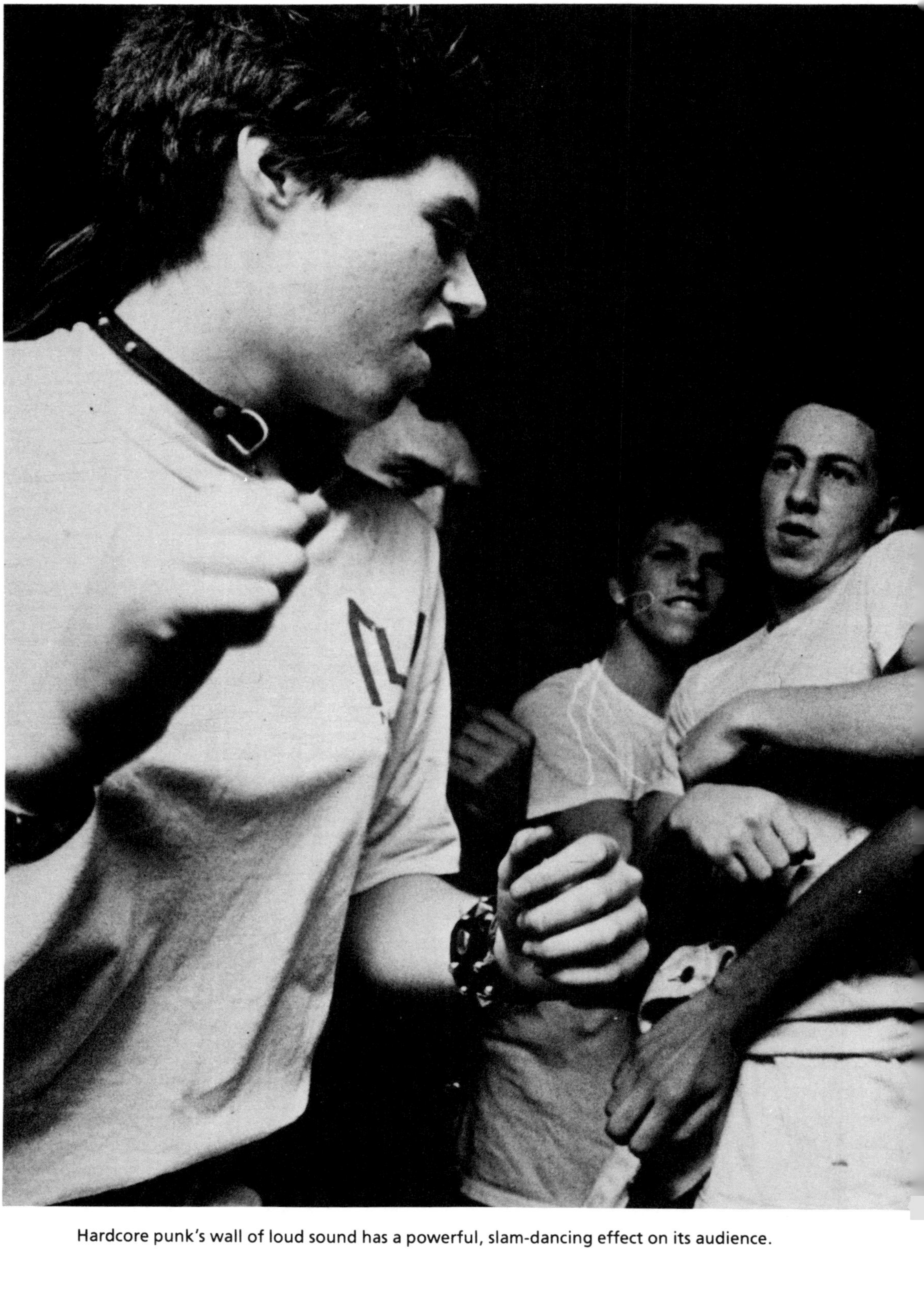

Hardcore punk's wall of loud sound has a powerful, slam-dancing effect on its audience.

Keri Pickett

of New Wave, "hard-core" punk groups held onto the youth and the purity of the wall of shrieking distortion, with some of the best groups made up of Americans from the Midwest, Washington, D.C., and Los Angeles.

Black Flag, from L.A. and Hüsker Dü, from Minneapolis, are probably the most finely untuned, longest-lasting, and well-toured of the current hard-core punk bands. Invariably, a hard-core "tune"—if you can call it that—lasts anywhere from thirty seconds to a couple of minutes, with all hell let loose at once at the loudest possible volume. The guitars are driven as if by saber saws with an occasional sustained discord; often the only harmonic changes are to alternate between two simple chords in a quick, two-beat per measure feel. Screaming voices mix in with the rest of the texture of the noise, and audience members get so worked up that their prickly shaved heads strain forward and their bodies pop up into the air, slamming sideways into each other or into the mikes on the front of the stage.

You could say that punk is rock stripped bare, all raw noise and aggressive energy. It was inevitable that it would be fitted into a minimalist format by young denizens of the downtown New York art scene who listened to Glass, Young, Reich, and Riley, and hung out at caves like CBGB's or Max's Kansas City. "Around 1977," recalls musician Glenn Branca, "there were a lot of young people in New York who grew up with rock and were also artists, who wanted to come and see something in a rock format but who also understood what art was. And it wasn't a matter of 'oh, this person is doing something pretentious, or something stupid to shock us'... they encouraged this kind of thing." It was an excited atmosphere which caused musicians to hyperactively mess around with distorted rock sounds, or as Tim Carr put it in *New York Rocker* (June 1982), "So there's another wave upon us. Splash! It is, as the editor of this mag told me, that Downtown Sound. It's been called Noise, art rock/rock art, skronk, rock concrete, post-modern no wave, a soundtrack for the apocalypse in progress, garage-punk-funk-jazz-electronic-communist white noise."

During this period Glenn Branca had come to New York from Boston, where he worked with an experimental theater company called Bastard Theater. He had played rock songs on guitar as a teenager, but started performing as an actor. He went into directing to better control what he was acting in, and then wrote plays so he would have better material to direct. His interest in music grew out of the composing he did for his theater pieces. From the beginning, he wanted to work with layered sounds. His earliest instruments were the cheap, small, reel-to-reel tape recorders he received as childhood presents. They would break easily and be replaced, so at one point he had three or four, and started "fooling around with them." For the theater, he worked with whatever he could find in the street or in pawn shops: chimes and gongs made of pot lids and other metals, a broken trumpet, and a melodica. He was never interested in rhythm; he liked to let things resound or sustain, and to build up textures. He got a hold of a Tanberg reel-to-reel recorder, recorded sounds from the outside world, and played with them by disengaging the gears of the recorder, trying to change the tape speed and vary the pitch, and making tape loops. With this and four-inch mouse amps (which could easily be distorted), he started to learn what he could do with sounds.

Branca's first exposure to modern experimental music came in the early 70s, while he was working in a record store, after he had begun exploring on his own. He didn't know what to listen to, and he kept asking customers who came into the store, "What's good?" Listening to Mahler for the first time, "I started hearing chords that sounded modern and said—'oh, wow!' " He went back with his new ears and heard similar material in Beethoven, then gradually worked his way to the twentieth century and finally to the back of the store where Glass, Reich, and Riley were.

Paula Court

Glenn Branca conducts horizontal, mallet-beaten guitars in a high-energy symphony.

With the excitement of the New York rock scene in progress in the mid-70s, Branca decided to form a rock band. Called Theoretical Girls, the band included Branca, Jeffrey Lohn, and Margaret Deuys, and "started off with twisted, punkish rock songs, then it exploded." A slew of ideas were tried out in front of club audiences. "The further out it was, the better they liked it . . . we were able to play in rock clubs because we packed the place."

Branca next formed the group The Static, so he could work towards his more personal ideas of "emotional structure." Each song expressed a different prototypical structure, in a very loud, very "visceral way, that made it very clear how the different building blocks were being used . . . I certainly saw it as entertainment, but you definitely had to work at it."

In 1979, Branca was invited to do a piece of his own at Max's Kansas City's Easter Festival, and he decided to try something that was just part of his chain of ideas. Called *Instrumental with Six Guitars,* it was a dense (twelve-minute-long) layering of minor third and second intervals (notes very close to each other) through the entire range of the guitars. He had the musicians strum back and forth in a way meant to obliterate rhythm; he wanted to create the most homogeneous sound possible. And at the first (very loud) rehearsal, "I heard something I never heard before. At the end of the piece, I had created what turned out to be a kind of massive field of chords. And it sounded absolutely amazing . . . I didn't know what I was hearing . . . It certainly wasn't something I had written. I didn't have the vaguest idea something like this could happen, if you want to know the truth. The moment I heard this, I knew I had to work with it." After a few more short sound fields like this one, working—as in his *The Ascension* with "the incredible variety of clusters," and "cluster movement"—Branca decided to write a full evening's performance, and he called it a symphony because that's the only word for a large-scale form with developing thematic ideas.

In his first couple of symphonies, Branca assembled his "guitar armies" and attacked the listeners for hours with deafening crescendos in various types of sonic organization, over the relentless backbeat versatility of drummer Stephan Wischerth. "I've been trying not to let go of the exciting aspects that I got from rock. It's always tempting to do something purely theoretical, but I don't want to do that." The rock drumming builds a vibrant sonic field of its own. "I don't want just a static chord . . . the drumming begins to break up the sound. And the drums do build up a visceral intensity; it is the only instrument that can do that."

Branca also built some original instruments for his symphonies. Horizontal, mallet-struck electric guitars give open-string resonance and tuning flexibility. Special electric harpsichords are made for microtonal tuning systems and have an extra bridge and displaced pick-ups to emphasize sympathetic vibrations of the strings. The *Symphony #2* also added the crash field artistry of Z'ev—a noise percussionist in his own right—who tortured large metallic assemblages while wearing S&M drag, naked to the waist, his head shaven.

Before creating *Symphony #3 (Gloria),* Branca had heard a lot about the harmonic series. But he didn't totally understand what it was until his girlfriend gave him a book by Dane Rudhyar, her favorite astrologer, called *The Magic of Tone,* which explained it clearly and with meaning, the way only a mystic could. (Actually, Rudhyar was a composer before he started writing about astrology). "A tone is a direct experience, but music is a myth," says Rudhyar, explaining one of the tenets of the book. A tone is, simply put, a sound of definite pitch. Harmonics are what make up a tone, and also what make the sound quality, or "timbre" of a violin different from that of a flute. Tones are made up of the fundamental—the strongest sound or the sound that gives the tone a certain pitch—plus the overtones—a series of sounds above the fundamental that go up mathematically. "The harmonic series considered as a series of intervals," writes Rudhyar, "is like a ladder whose rungs occur at always diminishing distances from one another." This ladder can be reversed, also, to form a descending harmonic series. With *Symphony #3,* Branca began using the harmonic series as a tuning system for his instruments. Instead of isolating the overtones, or making them more important than the fundamental like the "Harmonics" composers—LaMonte Young, David Hykes, Rhys Chatham, etc.—do, Branca's aim in playing the overtones as notes is to bring them all together to form one gigantic Sound, as Rudhyar would say in mystical parlance, a sort of reuniting of the multiplicity to form the One.

And it's a big One, in Branca's case. Using the concert hall as a huge sounding box, he blasts together the overtones for long, continuous periods. "The higher the volume, the longer the sound is maintained," says Branca, "the more the real character of the sound will become dominant, as a combination instead of separate tones." This phenomenon can only be heard in performance, and it's in performance that Branca hears what he's written for the first time. It's a risky way of operating, but it's true experimentalism. "Sometimes you'll have an absolutely dumb, boring, stupid experience one night and on the next night, with the same piece, you'll have the most wonderful, fluid, organic kind of quality."

To form the piece the way he wants it at a performance, Branca conducts the ensemble in an emotional way that's somewhere between cartoon "longhair" conducting and New Wave dancing. "I like to think of this sort of music affecting a fusion of mind and body, where the experience becomes total. Sometimes it fails on that level . . . but when it succeeds, it can be absolutely stunning."

Other innovators in the noisy New York experimentalism have been Rhys Chatham, with *Guitar Trio* (1977) and *Drastic Classicism,* and, on the rock side, Lydia Lunch with her group Teenage Jesus and the Jerks, and Arto Lindsey with DNA. Both Lindsey, who has been called James Brown trapped in Don Knotts' body, and Lunch, once called "a Billie Holiday nightmare," screech and scat their way over the mesh of grinding gears formed by their own untuned and strangled guitars and their lumpily driving bands. Both Lindsey and Lunch pioneered the short song length of noise bands—DNA's are the most compressed, often lasting less than thirty seconds—with very tight, breathtaking arrangements.

The classically trained Rhys Chatham turned to rock after searching for a popular idiom that would affect a mass audience. His works in the late 70s took very limited materials—single notes or jarring chords—and repeated them with rock guitar strumming and volumes. *"Drastic Classicism,"* says Chatham, "was a very dissonant piece, I'd say the grand-daddy of noise rock. On the tapes maybe it sounds very beautiful or like a vacuum cleaner, but at CBGB's—just imagine it—everybody's a little out of tune and the idea was don't turn that amp up to ten—turn it up to eleven! (Did you see the movie *Spinal Tap?*) I liked the energy, the aggression, the feeling of loud music—everyone did. For art spaces, we provided cotton balls for people to put in their ears . . . Actually, cotton balls don't do a damn bit of good. If you want to use something, use cigarette filters, just break them off and stick them right up there." Another reason for the high volume was to bring out overtones in the created noise field. Chatham wanted to make the overtones sing out and form their own rhythm against the 4/4 drumming, instead of having them merge into Branca's One Big Sound. "Kids would come up and say," Chatham remembers, 'where are the singers? I hear singers.' What they were hearing were the overtones."

For a while, the connection between the white-noise bands and minimalism was very clear. There was even an all-guitar version of Riley's *In C* played at an art gallery. But soon, dozens of bands sprang up, consisting mostly of untrained musicians who wanted to have a go at it, who strummed ear-shattering discords, yelled, and beat out tat-boom, one-two rhythms. The music was instantly disposable, an expression of nihilism and "anti-art within an art context" (Tom Paine of the band Live Skull). But there was also tremendous energy, lots of critical attention at three o'clock in the morning, and usually at least one good idea in each band. By the early 80s, there were enough bands working with noise to hold two festivals: the Noise Festival of 1981 and the Speed Trials of 1983, both taking place over several nights at White Columns, an art gallery/performance space located west of Soho in New York City. There was even a British glamour version of a noise band, with wide record distribution, and lead vocals by a notorious punk star: Johnny Lydon, the former Johnny Rotten of the Sex Pistols, fronts a band called Public Image Ltd., or PiL. In their metal box LP, *Second Edition,* and *Flowers of Romance,* (which came in a film reel container), there are what seem like slow-motion versions of Jefferson Airplane with Lydon singing in high, mournful monotones over the sparse crashes, guitar, bass, and violin noise which often forms itself into Arabic modes. Gang of Four is another British group with a noise format that has sold lots of records.

Both these prestige groups started to gain a recognizably funky, street-wise dance feel by

Seminal noise-guitarist Arto Lindsey is seen here leading his band, DNA, in a neatly condensed song.

1983. In fact, many of the original noise bands in New York got funky before they fell apart. But, with time and practice, the ones that kept with noise have become more tightly organized, though still strangely tuned. Part of their purpose is to shock, but now the more skilled performers can draw the audience to them before lashing out at them. Live Skull, for instance, has developed an intricate web of vocals, expert drumming, and dueling guitars. Lyrics, too, though still shrieked through the din, are more carefully composed and have more thought-out meanings.

Bands like Sonic Youth and Rat At Rat R think of their lyrics as poetry; much of it is political. Victor Poison-Tête, the lead singer of Rat At Rat R, accuses—like a Beat-era poet over the feedback of his electric violin. Both bands, however, are still very concerned with the types of sounds they produce; so experiment with distortion boxes during sets.

These bands also have a recognizable tendency to return to their Futurist origins and attempt to recreate the sound of the clamoring Industrial Revolution. In fact, industrial rock has become a small international movement. Swans, from New York, comes down with everything on a heavy one, one, one—like a pile driver—and their instruments include pipes, chains, and pieces of metal found in the street. Test Department, from Britain, is a cooperative of socially conscious noisemakers who stage multi-media events accompanied by the whirr and clang of machinery. And a German group whose name translates to mean Collapsing New Buildings (they're named in honor of a Berlin construction company whose buildings would collapse as soon as they were erected) has jackhammers and cement mixers on stage. These are some of the loudest bands in existence, and they seem to sustain the strain in rock that writer Albert Goldman noticed in the music of Jimi Hendrix in 1968: "Hendrix's program for the country blues was rural electrification. The end products were Futurist symphonies of industrial noise . . . clangorous sheet metal plants, whirring power stations . . . This new factory music brought the evolution of the blues full circle. Those famous laments had begun as labor pains: the field hand working alone in a Sahara of cotton would cry out to raise his spirits or purge his pain. Now a New Negro from the North had revived the primitive form by shouting ecstatically above the blind roar of the machine. That shout was an industrial arwhoolie."

Both percussion and distorted electric sounds have had wide play in sound exploration, but their emotional range is limited to anger, aggression, or a frenzy that combines the two. On the other hand, the role that the human voice plays in music—whether in "art" music or rock—is often used to express the gamut of emotions. Indeed, art-music experimentalists of the early twentieth century, in stretching the possibilities of the voice, sought to express the inner world and all its complexity. Not surprisingly, emotionally super-charged vocal explorations first occurred in the city where Sigmund Freud was exploring that inner world: Vienna. There, Arnold Schoenberg and Alban Berg developed the technique of *Sprechstimme,* an eerie, sometimes hysterical blend of speaking and singing, which they used in their vocal and operatic works.

As with new instrumental sounds, the range of vocal possibilities grew even broader after World War II. Many composers demanded amazing feats from the singers performing their music. Luciano Berio had such a close affiliation with one soprano who could sing his difficult pieces—Cathy Berberian—that he wound up marrying her, and composed most of his vocal works of the 60s and 70s specifically for her voice. Berio and like-minded contemporaries, such as Stockhausen and Penderecki, also placed demands on the audience as well, requiring them to unravel a complex and diffuse-sounding array of yawps, sighs, wails, screeches, whispers, teeth-and-tongue clicks, and so on. The mood of their pieces was intense and disturbing—dreamy at best, and often downright creepy. However, the ultimate emotional im-

The sounds of modern, poorly-designed construction is reproduced by Germany's Collapsing New Buildings.

Courtesy of Mute Records, U.K.

pact could be almost nil since the lack of rhythm and melody made the music hard for many people (especially Americans—Europeans seemed to like it more) to get into.

Nonetheless, emotive vocal expression can be presented with strong rhythm. This is the case with much of the rock music discussed here: from David Byrne with his paranoid tenor to the hard-core and noise bands who try to shriek their guts right out of their mouths. In pop music itself, a trend toward greater expression began in the 40s and culminated with rock. Frank Sinatra, for example, made his particular kind of crooning more emotional than Perry Como's style by stretching and cutting syllables according to his feelings. In early rock, yips, sighs, and gasps gave expression to the inexpressible. In fact, throughout the 60s it was the down-to-the-blues styles that carried the most personal emotion, as in the angst-ridden singing of Janis Joplin.

In pop experimental vocal music, emotion has usually been shunned. The voice parts written by Glass and Reich are cool and detached, using the clean, vibratoless pipe-voices of pre-romantic music. But when multimedia artist Meredith Monk heard Janis Joplin, she was pushed out of a year-long depression and back into her vocal explorations. "It was the rawness and the juiciness and that kind of visceral quality that Joplin had that made me want to work again," Monk says.

Meredith Monk represents the fourth generation of singers in her family—her great-grandfather was a cantor, her grandfather a bass who founded the Harlem school of music, and her mother a singer popular in early radio; in fact, Monk was born in Peru, where her mother was on tour. She was educated early in music theory, harmony, and piano, and sang a lot as a child. "I would have been a classical lieder (art song) singer, but I was never happy in that world. I wanted to find my own way of expression." At first she found it in dance, which she had also been studying since an early age. During her first year in New York, 1964, she was choreographing as well as dancing in theater works and avant-garde happenings. But then, returning to voice exercises, she started to play around and "realized," she says, "that the voice had the possibilities of as personalized a vocabulary as movement, and that it had the capacity to do many things." At first, Monk worked in a high register, sliding up and down and trying atonal progressions of vocal sounds, and also simple, chant-like lines. During this early experimentation she did a duet with voice and echoplex, an echo box which also distorts. She used a lot of material with "large intervals and fast changes . . . I was just working with my own voice and the particular qualities that it had; I wasn't thinking of any vocal models." She did record a sort of minimal psychedelic rock song, "Candy Bullets and Moon," that exists on a small pressing of the group Aunt Jemima and the United Pancakes (which included Monk and instrumentalist Robert Preston). Her voice wafts in and out in high, distorted monotones. *Juice,* Monk's first extended vocal score, had simple musical patterns for—as it was performed in New York's Guggenheim museum—violin, eighty-five voices, and eighty-five Jew's harps—those little metal instruments you put between your teeth and twang with your finger.

"Jew's harps really taught me about resonance in my mouth—a lot of things I do vocally came from working with them. Because the changes in the cavity of the mouth change the pitch and the qualities of the sound . . . you can do the same thing vocally. It's a wonderful instrument for a singer." Sitting cross-legged on the floor of her loft next to her pet turtle, Neutron, she demonstrates, putting a Jew's harp in her mouth and twanging it. "That's the fundamental tone; you always hear it . . . it's the essential drone instrument. Whatever you do with your mouth will get your overtone series." Still hitting the instrument, Monk pulls her upper lip over and forward like an awning, and higher tones are heard simultaneously with the

Gaetano Besana

Meredith Monk's vocal experiments often use the most simple materials in an adventurous spirit.

drone. She sings with the harp still in her mouth. It sounds like two people humming loudly.

In her group performances in the 70s and 80s, Monk developed a music of vocal sounds—the free, personal sounds of herself and her ensemble members—over simple, lulling, sweetly chorded electric piano accompaniment. Even without the visuals, pieces such as *Songs from the Hill* and *Tablet* contain an amazing array of emotions in this simple format without words. "Words are too compelling," Monk comments. "The subtle emotional palate is what I'm most interested in . . . the voice is a very powerful connection to feeling, even on a physical level—it comes from your gut, it comes straight up through your body, and it goes out your mouth. And I think society now is so systematically eliminating emotion, people are less and less comfortable with it. It's not cool. In a way, it's a sort of a stand, to make a music that makes a person in the audience remember what it is to have emotion . . . I remember going to a New Music festival where people would be leaving other performances looking like they'd just been drugged, and I was very happy to see people leaving our concert with their cheeks pink—they were awake."

There are others, especially women, who are plumbing the depths of their psyches through vocal sounds. Yoko Ono did it in the late 60s with ghostly glissandos; Joan LaBarbara in her latest album *Reluctant Gypsy* does it with scary, multilayered whispering. The most extreme is probably Diamanda Galas, who shrieks into a panoply of modifying equipment, taking near-mythic tragedies and historical outrages (like the slaughter of villagers under the recent Greek junta) as a starting point for her own, personal expression of sound.

In Felix Emmel's *Ecstatic Theater* (1924), a sort of manifesto of the German Expressionist theater (which developed Shriek Opera), the vocalizing actor is said to fall into two categories:

Diamanda Galas preparing for her Lincoln Center debut of psychic exploration.

Robin Holland

The first (as summarized by writer Richard Zvonar) is "the actor of nerves, whose performance was based on close observation of other individuals to create a finely-drawn psychological mosaic," and the second, "the actor of blood, whose changing stage persona was always rooted in his own internal reality, the unity and flow of his blood." It seems that while male vocalizers tend to imitate musical instruments and create psychological types (witness David Byrne's paranoid schizophrenic), recent female vocal experimenters have tended to fall into the category of "the actor of blood." Whether inner exploration is a trait from the "feminine" side of us all, or whether—in this post-feminist period—women are more interested in personal realization after eons of suppression, it is hard to say. It is clear, though, that the plaintive human cry needs to be heard among the roar of all that machinery.

Discography

George Antheil	BALLET MÉCHANIQUE	*Philips 6514254*
Erik Satie	PARADE	*Columbia M-30294*
Edgard Varèse	IONISATION	*Columbia Masterworks MS 6146*
Jimi Hendrix	ARE YOU EXPERIENCED?	*Reprise 6261*
The Ramones	ROCKET TO RUSSIA	*Sire 6042*
Black Flag	DAMAGED	*SST-Unicorn 9502*
Glenn Branca	THE ASCENSION	*99 Records 001*
Glenn Branca	SYMPHONY NO. 3 (GLORIA)	*Neutral Records N-4*
Lydia Lunch	QUEEN OF SIAM	*ZE 33006*
DNA	A TASTE OF DNA	*American Clavé 1003 EP*
Public Image Ltd.	SECOND EDITION	*Island 2WX 3288*
Sonic Youth	CONFUSION IS SEX	*Neutral Records 009*
Arnold Schoenberg	PIERROT LUNAIRE	*Nonesuch 71251*
Meredith Monk	SONGS FROM THE HILL	*Wergo Records 1022*
Diamanda Galas	DIAMANDA GALAS	*Metalanguage*

TAPE-SYNTH TECH

In the spotlight of a large concert hall, multi-media artist Laurie Anderson is silhouetted in front of projected graphics showing the derivations of Japanese pictograms. In front of her, taking up less space than a surfboard, is a machine capable of generating millions of sounds, distorting sounds in hundreds of unearthly ways, and storing collected sounds so they can be played instantly with the touch of a key. With this computer keyboard (with the brand name of Synclavier—shoppers should be warned that prices start above sixty thousand dollars), Anderson could mix a record on stage with information stored on twenty-four digital recording tracks. If she plugged into a printer, everything would be printed out in musical notation. "What I'm doing, basically," Anderson says, "is bringing a recording studio up on stage with me."

It's about time the recording studio took a bow. If there's any one thing that has revolutionized modern music, it's the ability to take sounds, store and modify them easily, and overlay them one on top of another. And if there's one thing that unites the pop experimentalists with rock music, it is the utilization of the recording studio along with synthesizers and new digital hardware and software as a primary composition tool.

Michael Putland/Retna Ltd.

Brian Eno, formerly of Roxy Music, has promoted the use of the recording studio as a composition tool and relies heavily on tape loops in his ambient music.

Recording was not always a creative process. From the late nineteenth century up until World War II, complete performances were actually scratched onto a master disc. Whether the process involved playing into a large cone that gathered the sounds to turn them into vibrations that scratched wax (Edison's early process), or into multiple microphones converging on an electromagnetic head that cut blank shellac master tapes, nothing could be changed once the recording had begun.

But in 1945, U.S. forces in Germany captured some Magnetaphons, a machine that used sound to rearrange magnetic particles on tape; in other words, the first practicable tape recorder. Now things could be changed on recorded performances. If Bing Crosby let a blue word slip on his radio show, it could be cut out; or everything except the best songs could be cut out and the best edited together.

Also, with two tape recorders, an instrument could be recorded on one machine, then played back, and an artist could sing with it, while the second recorder recorded the combined sounds. This added enormous flexibility to putting sounds together, although there was a problem: each time the sound was bounced from one tape recorder to another, the tape hiss would build. The solution was multitracking. Recorders that could divide recording tape into first two (stereo), then three parallel tracks of tape area that would record and playback in synchronization were developed. For instance, rhythm instruments were recorded on one track first, then melodic instruments on another, and then—while listening to the first two tracks—the vocals were recorded on top of that. The sound of each track could then be manipulated independently—filtering, adding echo, bringing up or lowering the relative volume of each tape—until, together, they sounded the way one wanted them to. Then, when the sound was perfect, all three tapes were mixed for a unified sound with the low tape hiss of a fresh recording.

This overlay of changeable sounds is the boon of multi-tracking, and it's advantages have remained the same as the number of tracks has multiplied. *Sergeant Pepper's Lonely Hearts Club Band* was recorded in 1967 on the standard four-track equipment of the time. Today, professional recording studios have machines that divide tape into 24 tracks, and include noise reduction systems to keep fidelity high and sounds crisp during the mixing process. The equipment has become smaller and less expensive too, so that even home recording studios today can, with the right know-how, produce amazing results. Digital recording, where sounds are computer-analyzed up to 50,000 times per second and then converted back to sound in various ways, is the ultra-modern way of doing the same thing.

The creative flexibility of the recording studio has made the producer, who oversees the complete recording and mixing process, and the engineer, who rules the mixing board, equal to the composer in degree of responsibility for what a piece of music sounds like. In fact, the producer is often the composer of a pop song. Pioneering producers include Les Paul, the guitarist and guitar inventor, who as early as 1948 bounced layers of sound back and forth between monaural tape recorders. He and Mary Ford went on to create, with early multitrack equipment in the 50s, lush textures within their duets. Sam Phillips of Sun Records gave Elvis Presley and Jerry Lee Lewis their deep echos. Phil Spector made multilayered cakes out of songs by the Ronettes and the Crystals, filling any cracks in his "wall of sound" with overdubbed violins, angel choirs, and shaking bells.

It seems like multitracking was used at first either for fixing mistakes (it's said that 60s teen idol Fabian often had to do up to a hundred takes in order to get enough acceptable material to edit together one song) or to add lushness. The first pop musical style in which the mixing board was widely used to create a clean, sparse multilayered effect typical of the modern well-produced song was Jamaican reggae. Through the mid-60s, Jamaican record producers such as Coxone Dodd and Lee Perry produced amazing results with one-track machines, or even direct-to-disk recording. When the first two-tracks reached the island in the late 60s, these producers were ready to take full advantage of them. Instead of just piling a lot of material on top of other material, they also subtracted a lot, creating open textures that let subtle polyrhythms, and each special effect—such as heavy echo—come through loud and clear. One immediate reason for this new technique of cutting out rather than merely adding on was the need to provide "dub" versions of singles for deejays to rap over.

The avant-garde were quick to take advantage of the possibilities opened up by tape recording. In the 40s, the Frenchman Pierre Schaeffer developed *musique concrete,* building collages of tape-recorded sounds from the outside world. The public debut of this new discipline was a *Concert of Noises* broadcast over French radio in 1948. After his exploration of tape recording, Schaeffer declared: "Photography, whether the fact be denied or admitted, has completely upset painting, just as the recording of sound is about to upset music." Schaeffer saw that music of the past was abstract, starting from written symbols; music of the future, with the new technology, must be concrete, starting with recorded sounds, whether instrumental or otherwise. Collaborating with composer Pierre Henri in the 50s, Schaeffer created a symphony, an opera, and an experimental studio for recorded music, which was used by avant-gardists such as Pierre Boulez, who thought that they better get to know what this new technology was all about.

Musique concrete was the beginning of a new field now known as electronic music. Another important area of this field is the electronic creation of new sounds. For a long time, there has been an interest in the mechanical creation of sounds; the player piano was the most successful example of a pre-electronic mechanical instrument. It wasn't until recently that the superhuman capabilities of the player piano were explored: Conlon Nancarrow, working in isolation in Mexico, composes directly on piano rolls, and has created dense, rhythmic sound pieces. But again, it was Edgard Varèse, in his quest to "liberate" sound, who first explored ways in which twentieth-century technology could increase the sounds available to art music, beyond those produced by the percussion instruments he had employed for *Ionisation*. Even the electronic instruments that appeared in the 20s—the Ondes Martenot, the Theremin, and the Trautonium—were too timid in their sonic liberation for the adventurous Varèse. "I refuse," he declared, "to limit myself to sounds that have already been heard. What I am looking for is new mechanical mediums which will lend themselves to every extension of thought and will keep up with thought."

In the 1930s, Varèse worked with engineers in the physical research department of Western Electric, in an attempt to realize some of those "new mechanical mediums." Unfortunately, his funding soon dried up. "We are here to improve the value of the investor's dollar," Western Electric's director of physical research, Harvey Fletcher, told the composer—evidently electronic music struck the board of directors as a losing proposition.

But in the early 50s things started looking up. Wartime advances in technology as well as booming postwar markets and increasing faith in technology all set the stage for new collaborations between composers and engineers. Large American corporations, such as Bell Labs and RCA, sensing that they could one day find sound synthesis useful, started intensive and wide-ranging research.

In the late 50s, engineers at RCA developed the Electronic Music Synthesizer. A synthesizer differs from an electric instrument—an electric guitar for instance, or a Fender-Rhodes-type electric piano—because it produces sound from pure electric current, whereas electric instruments start with vibrations of strings or metal plates that are turned into sound through amplification. In a synthesizer, voltage determines the various characteristics that make up a sound: a voltage-controlled oscillator sets the pitch; and filters and amplifiers, also voltage-controlled, determine the other characteristics of a sound, such as the overtones that give it a particular timbre. One very complex characteristic of a sound is the attack-and-decay envelope. This describes the way that a sound changes from the point at which the note is first hit until it dies away. A note hit on an acoustic piano, for example, starts out with a sharp attack and quickly fades, but the various overtones fade at different rates, making it a sound that's extremely complicated.

Today, with the rapid advancement of computer components used to control the various sound characteristics, it's much easier to program a complex sound into a synthesizer. But in the early days of synthesizer development, there was a lot of manual cord-plugging and dial fiddling. At one point, complex sounds were programmed on punched paper, much like player-piano rolls. Still, with synthesizers, composers are now able to electronically produce

In the Columbia-Princeton Electronic Music Center (l to r): Mario Davidovsky, Pril Smiley, Arthur Kreiger.

The Columbia-Princeton Electronic Music Center

any tones they want, and to make that tone as loud or soft, sharp or mellow, long or short as seems effective.

With the advancement of sound synthesis and multitrack technology, the music departments of prestigious American universities—notably Columbia and Princeton—became interested in electronic music. In 1959, a large grant established the Columbia-Princeton Electronic Music Center, dedicated to "facilitate the task of composers desiring to compose with the expanded sound resources available on magnetic tape or needed to be built up through sound synthesis," as the charter stated. A short time later, the center obtained the most

Vangelis composes imaginative synthetic albums and movie soundtracks.

Frank Driggs Collection

advanced model of the RCA sound synthesizer, the Mark II. Soon composers working at the center—Milton Babbitt, Vladimir Ussachevsky, and Otto Luening—were all offering complex blends of amplified blurps, fwipps, simps, twings, and schlonks. These sounds, spooky yet somehow cool and cerebral, darted from speaker to stereophonic speaker in auditoriums where listeners sat staring into space, since there were often no human performers to speak of. The sounds were either *musique concrete,* natural sounds that were altered beyond recognition, or else totally synthetic sounds. In some pieces, the taped sounds stood on their own; in others, they would be combined with music by live players.

At the same time that these American composers were writing pioneering electronic pieces, European composers were also setting out for new technological frontiers. The German Karlheinz Stockhausen availed himself of the electronic generators at Radio Cologne to compose his *Der Gersang der Jünglinge,* and went on to create vast aural tapestries—such as *Hymnen* and *Momente*—that relied, at least in part, on electronics. Luciano Berio, Ilhan Mimaroglu, and Iannis Xenakis also concocted strange hi-tech brews as exotic-sounding as their last names.

As for Varèse, the father of them all, he too finally got the long-awaited opportunity to create the sort of music he had been hearing in his head for years, with the electronic sequences in *Desérts,* and *Poème Eléctronique.* In these works, the maverick composer hoped to create what he termed an "atmospheric disturbance." As his biographer Fernand Ouellette recalls, "the sounds did, in fact, do violence to the listener's body," intending the remark no less disparagingly than it would sound coming from a Led Zeppelin fan. Less sonically overwhelming in his electronic music than Varèse, in the mid 50s, John Cage often used tape recorders while composing such pieces as *Variations II.*

With its emphasis on sonic texture, and lack of easily discerned rhythm, repetition, variation, development, and (God forbid) melody, this early electronic music had the same problem as other avant-garde music of its time—it never won large audiences, at least not in the U.S. and Britain (continental Europeans, however, seemed more intrigued by it). It was the kind of music that made cats' ears prick up with curiosity, that thrilled human ears with the new sonic perspectives it revealed, and that, with its multitracked, chaotic sound, mirrored the complexities and simultaneous sounds of daily life in the modern world. However, after limited exposure, it put most listeners to sleep, although an uneasy one.

Technology gallops ahead, though, and it wasn't long before completely electronic music was producible outside of the academic labs. Around 1964, Robert Moog invented a synthesizer that could be produced commercially, and by 1968 a model was practicable enough for a full album of Bach transcriptions. *Switched-on Bach,* released that year, served to popularize the electronic sound for mass audiences. The Bach inventions, preludes, and concertos were realized by Walter Carlos (now Wendy Carlos due to a sex-change operation) on a Moog 55 that was set up in modular units connected together with cords. Sounds could take hours to construct, and had to be layered on tape, sometimes phrase by phrase, a laborious task that would be laughed at by the modern computer synthesist. But the result was a palpable electronic "feel" that took such a joy in itself (and in Bach), that it is almost earthy, though Carlos does take some liberty on the album to explore, if not outer space, then at least a twenty-first-century sewage treatment plant in the improvised cadenza of the Third Brandenburg's second movement. The wide variety of timbres employed by Carlos give a wonderful clarity to Bach's use of counterpoint (the rhythmic interplay of voices) without getting too caught up in the use of the new sounds for their own sake. Because of this, Carlos' use of the synthesizer is a model for the intelligent use of electronics in any modern music, whether art music or pop. Carefully employed, synthesizers can provide exciting clarity of contrasting timbres in the multilayered collages of new sounds, and bring out the interplay of complex rhythms. In the early 70s, when truly portable stage synthesizers first came out, rock groups did not use this new technology in an intelligent way. British "art rock" groups such as Yes, Procol Harem, and Emerson, Lake and Palmer used synthesizers as flashy string sections; early music from the German group Kraftwerk had the same vague romantic effect with its cosmic sound. Connie Plank, a German producer who worked with many of the early German synthesizer bands and now mixes electronics for British synth-pop bands such as Killing Joke and Ultravox, thinks that perhaps synthesized sound is just not good for instrumental, semi-improvised rock 'n' roll. Much of it sounds, he said in a recent radio interview, "like projections into outer space, into very clean space. And I think that when you put music into such an area . . . it has no secret anymore."

A whole generation of synthesizer whizzes hovers near this cosmic emptiness, sometimes breaking into the real world, often staying somewhere between musical genres. The most notable of these hi-tech virtuosos, gleaming and glamorous, are Vangelis, Giorgio Moroder, Isao Tomita, Jean-Michel Jarre, Thomas Dolby, and Peter Gabriel. The last two have found the most success working in a rock idiom. Vangelis and Moroder have done extremely well with film soundtracks. In addition, Vangelis has done a wide range of more personal work, and sometimes hits notes of true poignancy when he mixes acoustic instruments with his machinery, as he does in *China*. Jean-Michel Jarre's most interesting work mixes in real sounds such as human voices, which he does extensively on the album *Zoolook*. But all these artists have a way of losing their tethers to the mother ship when dealing with synthesized tones alone.

The same lost-in-space problem exists in that "New Age" music of Eastern descent, much of which depends heavily on synthesizers and on "delays," electronic devices that repeat phrases after they are played, letting them fade out like mournful echos. Plank calls the dense and spacey use of synthesizers "psychedelic." The lush arrangements of the art/rock groups and the delay loops of the New Age electronics composers, who seem totally absorbed in their circuit world, certainly remind one of the drug culture of the 60s slowly burning itself out.

But the development in the late 70s of drum machines and sequencers (which create driving rhythms out of synthesized sounds) brought the beat to techno-pop. At the same time, the disco phenomenon created a whole new genre of dance music that was inspired by heavily rhythmic black rhythm 'n' blues. The new dance music, both R 'n' B and New Wave, created a less self-absorbed context for synthetic sounds and multitracked sound layering. "Synthesized sounds for disco music is fantastic," continues Plank.

One of the earliest bands to make all-electronic dance music was The Human League, which was formed in 1977 by two shift foremen of a computer company near Sheffield, England. By 1981, they had both their technology and their sensual dance format down, and made their first dance floor hit—"Don't You Want Me." A truce between technology and human emotion was formed by Eurythmics, whose "Sweet Dreams (Are Made of This)" puts the insistently repeating, minor-key vocals of Annie Lennox over the synthesizers of Dave Stewart.

It seems, though, that the most vital contexts for electronic sounds start with something concrete—a real artifact or "photograph" of sound as Pierre Schaeffer described it—which is then recombined, altered, or even destroyed. That's why poorer technologies often spark the best styles since they offer less opportunity to create sounds from scratch. It's not surprising, then, that exhilarating electronic sounds have come out of the South Bronx of New York City. Here, disc jockeys, such as Grandmaster Flash, hooked twin turntables to a mixer and com-

Syndication International/Photo Trends

The Eurythmics is one of the new generation of synth-pop groups to humanize technology.

bined records together, creating a sort of on-the-spot multitracking Like reggae, this music demanded a wide-open texture for rappin' deejays to chant over, as well as an infectious, fragmented rhythm for breakers to dance to. Sounds already on the records were augmented rhythmically by techniques such as "scratching," in which a record is pushed back and forth manually while the needle is still in the groove. Afrika Bambaataa, the head of the "Zulu Nation" of deejays, rappers, and breakers, began doing some of the most eclectic mixes, using TV show themes, disco music and manually-generated noise. After the gold hits of the Sugarhill Gang's "Rapper's Delight" and Bambaataa's "Planet Rock" (made over a Kraftwerk electronic track), "hip-hop" music—as the rap tracks are known—was successful enough to go hi tech. Drum machines were programmed to create sparse, but complex rhythms, sometimes booming on offbeats, sometimes gunning like only a machine can. Any sounds on top of the drum machines were used significantly, like "stings."

Some of the hottest electronic producers around have used the hip-hop feel to create dazzling electronic sound collages out of rock songs. Englishman Trevor Horn, for example, with his Zang Tumb Tuum record company (the name came from an Italian Futurist's description of the sound of a machine-gun noise), produced the *Art of Noise* album which included hypnotic hip-hop rhythms with effects, such as grinding auto transmissions, layered on top. With his sense of a clear, rhythmic texture, dramatic use of synthesizers, and earthy feel for funny sounds and timbres, Horn, with the group Frankie Goes to Hollywood, created Britain's biggest hit of 1984, "Relax." He often collaborates with Malcolm McLaren on his hip-hop sound collages such as the LP *Duck Rock,* and has been brought in to clarify many a murky-sounding record; he reworked Yes' "Owner of a Lonely Heart," for example, adding effects like one he calls "shoot the moose". The New York-based performing and producing group, Material, has, in the same way, given a street-tech feel to some American artists and their music, such as Herbie Hancock, who they blasted to the top of the charts with the song "Rock It."

Like the hip-hop dance music, pop experimentalists music seems to get most inspired by technology that's one step behind the times, technology that's no longer "the latest thing." Slightly out-of-date items, after all, make solid pop objects. Laurie Anderson prefers older drum machines because of their "cheesy" quality that reminds her of clocks ticking. Older technologies can also be manipulated more easily. One case, at least—Steve Reich's disturbed tape loops of the mid 60s (in an era when synchronized multitracking already existed)—suggested a path of rhythmic experimentation that Reich kept to in his later, non-electronic music.

"I remember it seemed disappointing that tape music, or *musique concrete,* as it was called, usually presented sounds that could not easily be recognized, when what seemed interesting to me was that a tape recorder recorded real sounds like speech, as a motion-picture camera records real images," writes Reich in his essay, "Notes on Compositions, 1965-1973." Reich combined his interest in recorded speech with an interest in intense rhythm through relentless repetition, which was nurtured when he worked on the first performance of Terry Riley's *In C,* in 1964. That year, Reich recorded a black preacher in San Francisco's Union Square ranting about impending doom. He took the words "it's gonna rain" and made tape loops which repeated these three words over and over again, and tried playing two identical loops against each other in various ways. When he tried playing both loops in unison, one was slightly faster than the other, and an amazing thing occurred. The shifting relationships set up a process that created ever-changing rhythms, from unison in the beginning to an echo, to a staccato battleground when the two loops were radically out of phase, gradually returning to the unison, when the words could again be clearly understood.

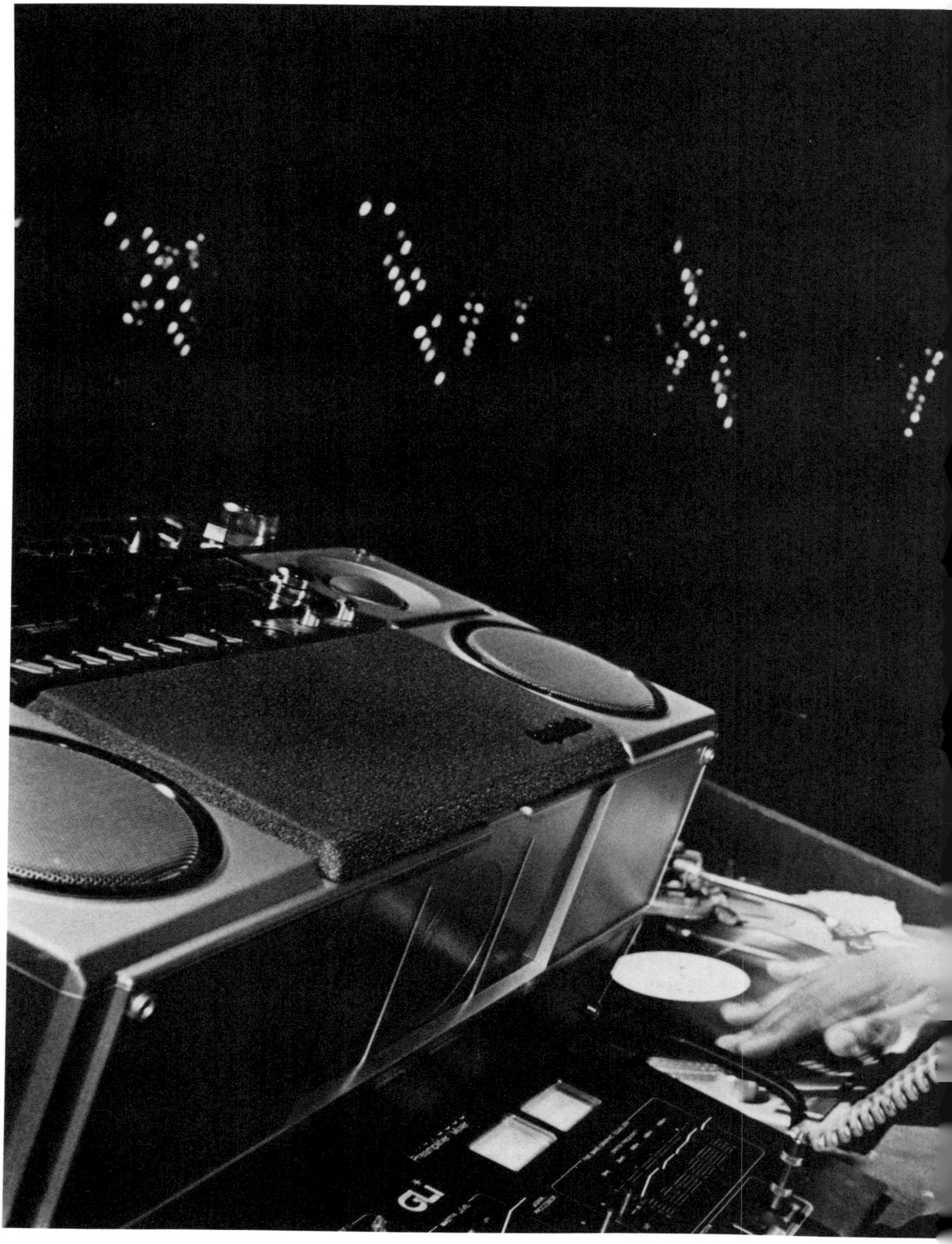

Afrika Bambaataa scratches a record into an original collage at the Roxy in New York.

Paula Court

Reich refined this process with two tape-loop pieces in 1966, *Come Out* and *Melodica.* He then decided to write music for live performers based on the phase-shifting process or "phasing," as it began to be called. In 1967, working with pianos and tape loops, he and a friend learned to gradually speed up against each other without any electronic aids, and *Piano Phase* was born. Reich had found a rhythmic structure for instrumental music which he would have never come to, he says, "by listening to any other Western, or for that matter, non-Western music. The question may then arise," he continues, "as to what it is like to imitate a machine while playing live music? I believe there are human activities that might be called 'imitating machines,' but which are, in reality, simply controlling your mind and body very carefully as in Yoga breathing exercises." Percussionist David Van Teighem, who played in Reich's 1971 phase piece, *Drumming,* says that, instead of feeling mechanical, phasing is exhilirating, and "has more in common with rock energy than anything else."

In 1968 and 1969, Reich designed a machine called the Phase Shifting Pulse Gate, which he abandoned after "it proved to be musically uninteresting in performance. I felt very clearly then that I did not wish to have any involvement with electronic music again." Reich kept to that feeling and in the mid-70s had even abandoned phasing. "It's a technique that no culture in the world uses and that no musicians in the world are trained to play. I wanted to start writing music that performers outside my ensemble could play."

Reich eventually found a way to get back to music that could be played by professional musicians, and to still retain the rhythmic intensity of phasing. He followed the examples of African, Indonesian, and Hebrew musics. But the phasing experience continues to figure in all of Reich's work through the use of canons. A canon is a musical device in which one part imitates exactly what another part is doing, for example, a round of "Row, Row, Row Your Boat." Reich's recent work, such as *The Desert Music* (1984), though written for standard orchestral ensembles and very playable by the average professional musician, retains the quirky and variable use of canons, reminiscent of the tape-loop phasing. And, to compose these overlapping canons, he uses an eight-track recording machine in his small studio, playing parts on top of each other to hear how they sound before he writes them out.

Other composers use high technology to enable live musicians to do things they'd never be able to do without its aid. Glenn Branca, for example, is writing choral music (as part of an opera projected for 1986) that requires singers to hit notes in an alien tuning system. This would be an impossible feat, except that the singers will wear earphones that will sound synthesized tones that they will then be able to duplicate with their voices.

In record production, pop experimentalists feel free to use the recording techniques of the rock world. Normally, classical music is recorded in much the same way as it was before the multitrack revolution: The orchestra is set up in the correct sonic environment, miked, and a piece is played through from beginning to end a few times. The best parts of each run-through are then edited together.

Kurt Munkacsi, long-time technical director of the Philip Glass Ensemble, has a completely different view of how music should be recorded. "I'm not interested in making a sonic photograph of the piece as it would be played in a concert hall," he says. Instead, he treats a record as a different entity from the live performance, something that stands on its own.

With Glass' opera, *Satyagraha,* Munkacsi started with a computer-generated click track that laid out rhythmic pulses for the piece. This was more difficult for Glass' music than one would assume. "Everybody thinks Philip's music just repeats over and over, but that's not really the case," he says. "The figures actually change in a way that's not regular to the computer." So they couldn't just set a tempo and let the computer run, the track had to be tediously adjusted to accommodate the rhythmic changes. And for two-against-three polyrhythms, there had to be two, sometimes three, click tracks running at once. A vocal cue track was laid over the click track, consisting of a voice saying things like "figure 39, repeat one, 39-two," etc., in order to tell the singers where they were in the score. Also against the click track, a "keyboard guide track" was constructed. The "keyboard guide track" was the basic score played on an electric keyboard by musical director and conductor Michael Reisman. While listening to these guides, the instrumentalists and singers recorded their parts in stereo, one at a time or in small groups. They repeated their parts until the optimal track was obtained.

After the acoustic recording was finished, Munkacsi used synthesizers to create the ideal sound for each instrument. In the case of the double bass, for example, they cut out all the bass sound and replaced it with a full-range synthesized bass, producing a rumble as low as 30 to 35 cps (cycles per second). What they wound up with was the rich sound of an acoustic bass plus the powerful low range of a synthesizer.

Glass, of course, has found that electronic instruments are very useful in his ensemble's live performances, where he uses both electric organs (which produce their sounds with vibrating coils instead of pure voltage coils) and synthesizers. "There's a great difference among electronic instruments," says Michael Reisman, "both in the way the sounds are produced and the resulting sounds." Reisman's left hand, playing a bass synthesizer, is the cohesive force in the group's sound. He found his ideal instrument in an early Arp model, which "is very limited—only a single voice, a single oscillator, and a single envelope generator—but it can produce four simultaneous wave forms and chorusing of four possible octaves." Using all the wave forms at once with the chorusing creates the "very fat sound" characteristic of the bass parts in the ensemble. Unfortunately, this instrument is not replaceable, since it went out of production long ago and very few of them were made in the first place. And it tends to break down since "it's in a small, light case and gets thrown around a lot."

Reisman, a composer himself and somewhat of a tech aficionado, with the aid of computer programmer Steven Buchwalter, has also made forays into the musical possibilities of that high-speed gamesman, the home computer. Their creation, Cantus, is a program for the Commodore 64, an inexpensive home system that has a built-in synthesizer. The program allows the operator to set the parameters—limit the ingredients—of a piece of music, such as the kind of harmonies, note lengths, tempos, etc. The probabilities of a certain kind of note or rhythmic factor appearing can also be set. Then, the computer will improvise endlessly within these limits, creating a flow of vibrant background music with little predictable structure, but a very definite character. "It gives me ideas for composing," says Reisman, "but you can't really compose on it since, after a certain point, it does what it wants to."

Wariness of computers and other hi-tech equipment that may take you where it wants you to go is not unusual among pop experimentalists. "I thought, at one point, maybe I should take two years and learn about electronics," says Laurie Anderson. "But then I was scared to do that. I thought in the end I might forget what I wanted to learn it for." Even though Anderson's Synclavier can concoct anything, she rarely uses its synthesized sounds. Instead, she prefers to "sample," or digitally record, real sounds—mostly words—through the machine, alter them, and play them back through the keyboard as part of the continual magic of her shows and the surprising textures of her songs. Engineers at New England Digital, the makers of the Synclavier, designed a violin interface for her so that the bowed and fingered strings will also call forth the digitally stored sounds, providing a different sort of visual magic as she produces natural and surprising noises from her violin. She can also conjure up unique music with a harmonizer, which can take sounds and raise or lower them as much as

Kurt Munkacsi's mixing board is an integral part of the amplified Philip Glass Ensemble.

Paula Court

four octaves. In live performance, she uses the harmonizer to lower her voice about an octave and a half so that when she speaks she seems inhabited (à la Linda Blair) by a smooth-talking shoe salesman. At one point in her performance, Anderson might also knock her forehead to produce a resounding boom, from contact with mikes embedded in eyeglass temples.

The viewer delights in these tricks the way one might enjoy the lower-tech sound explorations of David Van Teighem. They are seen as a "found" technology, picked out of the piles and piles of devastatingly new machines, doomed to quick obsolescence, that modern industry is driven to come up with each year. Anderson's is a fitting response to this hi-tech environment, and a caveat, too, to composers who would devote themselves to blindly following the glittering path of newer and newer microcircuitry.

Discography

Various Artists	PHIL SPECTOR WALL OF SOUND	*Phil Spector International (1981)*
Bob Marley and the Wailers	IN THE BEGINNING	*Trojan TRLS 221*
Conlon Nancarrow	COMPLETE STUDIES FOR PLAYER PIANO, Volume Two	*Arch Records 1750 S-1777*
Columbia-Princeton Electronic Music Center	TENTH ANNIVERSARY ALBUM	*CRI SD 268*
Walter Carlos	SWITCHED-ON BACH	*Columbia MS7194*
Vangelis	CHINA	*Polydor PD-1-6199*
Jean-Michel Jarre	ZOOLOOK	*Disques Dreyfus FDM 18118*
Grandmaster Flash, Melle Mel, et. al.	STREET BEAT	*Sugarhill Records SH-2-9228*
Afrika Bambaataa, et.al.	BEAT STREET	*Atlantic 80134-1*
Trevor Horn and Art of Noise	INTO BATTLE WITH THE ART OF NOISE	*Island DMD 744*
Steve Reich, et. al.	NEW SOUNDS IN ELECTRONIC MUSIC	*CBS Odyssey Records 32-16-1060*

NEW CON- TEXTS

Listening to music today is not what it used to be. "I'm from the first generation of composers who have grown up hearing music first on a record then, maybe later, in a concert hall," says Steve Reich. When you try to visualize where you've first heard a piece of music today, you might remember a highway divider flashing by, a tinny transistor radio on a camping trip, a friend's apartment with the cellophane wrapping of a new record littering the floor, or Ed Sullivan's "really big show" flipping on a TV screen. "You know, it's the music in the beginning of *2001*," someone might say, referring to a great late-nineteenth-century symphonic masterpiece coming over an elevator loudspeaker.

"The music created today is new and exciting," crowed Murray the K in 1966. "The music itself is far ahead of its manner of presentation on both radio and TV. New lyrical attitudes and new musical sounds have been found by today's writers and record producers. It is now up to radio disc jockeys and TV show producers to advance their presentation of this new musical expression. In other words, radio and TV must find a new frame of reference for today's music explosion."

Beatriz Schiller

The Kitchen was an industrial loft before it became a performance space and featured Philip Glass, Steve Reich, LaMonte Young, and many others.

Where does the concert hall fit into all of this? "It's an anachronism," says Robert Ashley, video opera composer/director. "A thousand people sit in a concert hall and wonder why they're there—'hey, wait, we did this 150 years ago, not now.' It became boring for me to go to a concert, sit there for the required amount of time, and then go out for coffee."

Of course, this sentiment is not universal among today's pop experimentalists. The interaction between performer and audience is often highly valued, as is the physical space where the interaction occurs. Glenn Branca uses a hall as a "huge sounding box" for example; Laurie Anderson often shapes her works around the location where they are to be presented. But it is no longer taken for granted that the concert situation is the best way to present something. Indeed, for those who grew up hearing music at home on stereos, on a radio in the car, at the Fillmore in San Francisco, or The Electric Circus in New York, or at Woodstock, the ritual of concert-going has become a big bore. In a society that likes to spend its leisure

Robert Ashley's mild-mannered voice and presence lend a relaxing air to his video opera, *Perfect Lives.*

Paula Court

time being physical, sitting at a concert with hands folded politely in the lap is less appealing than dancing in front of a rock stage and clapping in time when the lead singer screams "Everybody put your hands together!" Concert-going is less "active" than tooling along a freeway to the Beach Boys or talking to your roommate with a cassette of Stravinsky's *Petrouchka* blaring in the background. From the late 40s on, music has been associated with doing things. And the more portable it became, thanks to all the audio equipment that started flooding the consumer market after World War II, the less young people flocked to those straightlaced, non-participatory concerts in concert halls.

In addition, during the 50s America was on the move in a way, and at a speed, that no European nation had ever been. Young families were fleeing to the suburbs, people were zooming along highways—thousands of miles of new ones each year—in fast-moving cars. In suburbia, many people spent a good part of the day in cars, for there was no other way to get places. But all that moving around must have felt good because, when a music that you could not listen to *without* moving—hard-hitting, early rock 'n' roll—started to be heard, kids, raised as pleasure-loving consumers, went for it in a big way.

The old European tradition of concert-going, on the other hand, provided much less instant gratification. Compared to rock concerts, the atmosphere was prim and uptight, and the music, whether it was as accessible as Mozart or as tough to listen to as Webern, made demands on the audience, not vice versa. The listener could not just move to it; he or she had to listen hard. But a rock concert was easy, interactive listening all the way. And listening was just part of a band's performance. There was the movement, the raw physical presence of the crowd, the impromptu dancing, the drug taking, the loud cheering, the interaction between performers and audience—all of which would have been terribly out of place in the Palace of the Fine Arts in San Francisco.

The recognition of the importance of the setting has led many pop experimentalists to present their music in, or conceive it for, environments less traditional than the concert hall. New spaces to play in included the alternative music venues that sprang up in the early 70s—places like The Kitchen in New York City's SoHo district, and The Roundhouse in London. These were often located in areas not associated with official high culture. The neighborhoods were gritty, the decor of the playing spaces—often converted industrial lofts or storefronts—spare. Yet an air of modern-day pioneering prevailed with bare plank floors, exposed pipes, crumbling molding, and windows covered with Saranwrap in winter. These places were devoid of the gilt, the plush velvet, the glistening chandeliers, the tuxedoed musicians, the pompous conductor, or the weight of the past that traditional concert halls symbolized. Instead, seats were foam rubber-pads, and the musicians, dressed no differently than the audience, genuinely got into their music. Members of the audience could walk around or stretch out on the floor, head resting on a friend's lap. And though you weren't driving a car, the music was so steady, fast-paced, and rhythmic that, if you closed your eyes, it wasn't hard to pretend you were.

Not that the use of alternative spaces such as these was always a matter of choice. "I was a kid right out of college," says composer Rhys Chatham, who founded the Kitchen's music program in 1971. "Where was I going to play? Carnegie Recital Hall? But it was 200 bucks to rent it. And I thought, 'this sucks, it's ridiculous.' So I was collaborating with these two video artists, named Woody and Steina Vasulka, and they had just founded a place called the Kitchen Center [now The Kitchen] and I said, 'Why don't you do weekly concerts there?' The first person I asked to perform there was Philip Glass, but he had gotten to a point where he had to have a certain amount of money for his musicians and . . . we had a door situation [a common financial arrangement in new music venues: the musicians get a percentage of admission fees]." Eventually, Chatham managed to get arts grants, and Glass, Reich, and LaMonte Young could play there. Other early Kitchen performers included Jon Gibson, Music Electronica Viva, Phil Niblock, Frederic Rzewski, and Laurie Speigel. "Composers were allowed to do whatever they wanted, and they did just that," recounts Chatham. One composer named Maryanne Amacher even played a piece in Boston and 50 people sat in the Kitchen and tried to hear the piece telepathically (Chatham interjects: "This was right after the 60s, remember"). Two people claimed they heard it. "We made it a very relaxing atmosphere; no one was too self-conscious."

Two years later, CBGB, the prototype for the new-music performance underground rock club, opened on the Bowery in New York. Max's Kansas City, a familiar arena for the Velvet Underground, had existed earlier, but did not evolve to the type of punk and art atmosphere of flexibility that began at CBGB. It's full name, CBGB-OMFUG, originally stood for "Country, BlueGrass, and Blues—Other Music for Uplifting Gormandizers," but by 1974 the bar had become the place for spawning punk and New Wave groups. The Ramones, Television, and Debbie Harry all appeared there early in their careers; later, art/noise rockers like Rhys Chatham and Glenn Branca shook the house. To this day, there are late-night programs and weekend matinees featuring both hard-core and experimental bands (though usually not in the same show) that no one has ever heard of. The mood of the place, as well as the look—a sort of anteroom to a subway tunnel, with bar—has been repeated all over downtown New York, and throughout the U.S. and Europe. In New York's East Village, the latest bars of this type—the Pyramid Club, 8 B.C., and the Limbo Lounge—keep getting pushed further and further east as the central area becomes more civilized and upper-middle-class. According to the unofficial laws of economics, the frontiers of music often develop in the wild frontiers of crime-ridden urban areas.

In the late 70s, more glamorous versions of these clubs, such as the Mudd Club and later Danceteria, began to appear, but the mood—despite the attendance of higher-rent types, along with the anti-establishment crew—remained more casual than the loft-style alternative spaces. People danced, talked, drank, smoked, made out, got high, cruised, or just stood off to the side and got into music that sounded like rock except when you listened closely.

As quick as pop experimentalists were to branch out into new performing contexts, the commercial music industry expanded even more quickly. Today, the dissemination of music that started in the 50s has reached gigantic proportions. There is music everywhere: joggers and pedestrians are crowned with Walkmen, muzak arrangements resound through offices and stores; when you are on hold on the phone, you are treated to canned hits; kids tote "ghetto blasters" wherever they go, blaring them at top volume. The affluent have their car tape decks and radios, not to mention their home media centers. And there is the only slightly less omnipresent rock video, seen in discos, rock clubs, record stores, and on MTV—the latest territory annexed by the music business.

In some ways, all this conjures up images of high capitalism in an inflationary period, when the market is constantly flooded with tempting new commodities, and consumers must keep buying in an attempt to stave off financial collapse. In other ways, though, it can be seen as the fulfillment of the wish composers of art music have had for years: to fill the world with music. Of course, art-music composers were not the first to think in these terms. Most familiar are street musicians, who have been around for centuries, without getting too theoretical about their performance. Their singing and playing grabbed people's attention for a few minutes, then mixed with the noises of the environment as the listener moved on.

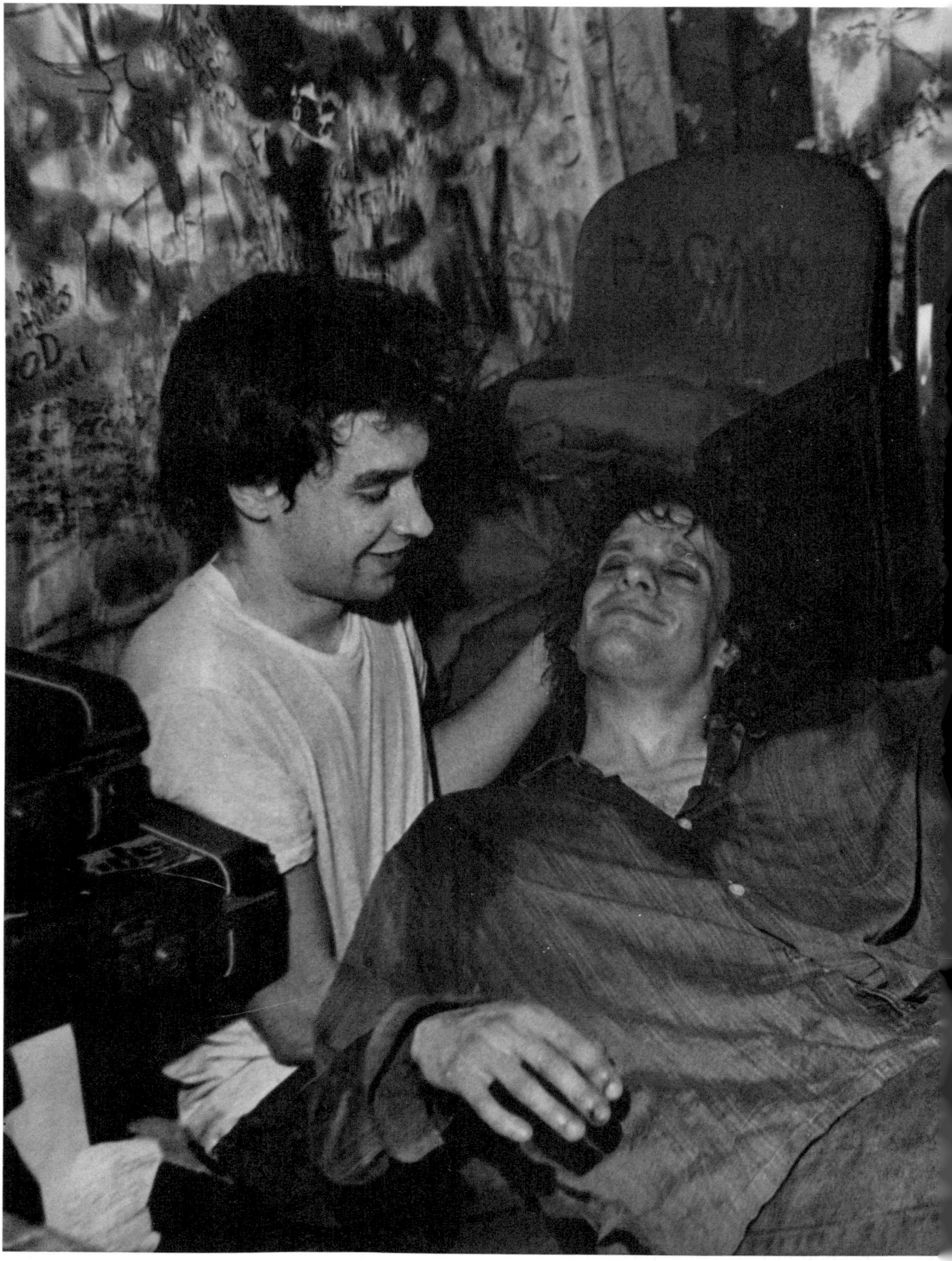

Four habitués of the New York City club, CBGB's, get into the easy-going, raucous mood.

Keri Pickett

As early as the turn of the century, some art music composers felt serious music had a place outside of the concert hall. The Russian composer Alexander Scriabin, for instance, dreamt up a mighty, seven-day-long extravaganza call *Mysterium* (and later given the more modest title of *Prefatory Action*). The piece was to be performed not in a hall or theater, but in a huge, specially built temple in India, with a semicircular wall mirrored in a reflecting pool. A victim of sexual and egomaniacal excesses, Scriabin did not consider his hopes that *Prefatory Action* would spiritually transform the world out of line. Sadly enough, he died before he was able to complete the score.

Erik Satie and Darius Milhaud's so-called furniture music provides a total contrast to Scriabin's grandiose scheme. Created in 1920, it was made up of repeated bits of pop and operatic hit tunes of the day. Satie and Milhaud meant it to be played during intermission of a surrealistic play performed in an art gallery, while the audience walked around looking at pictures. Unlike Scriabin, they were not attempting to change people with their music. In fact, they announced, "We beg you to take no notice of it, and to behave during the entr'actes as if the music did not exist." In his biography of Satie, Rollo Myers tells how it irked the composer when people actually paid attention to the bland proto-Muzak; he insisted that they chat and make noise instead.

It is not likely that Scriabin, Satie, and Milhaud could forsee the future for art music that blended with daily life. And yet, in America by 1934, the company "Music by Muzak" piped pleasant arrangements of pop and light classical tunes into working places and shops as a way to boost productivity or buying. "Whatever you do, don't listen," a recent *New York Times* article quotes the company's current Director of Communications—a man after Satie's heart if ever there was one—as saying.

Today, Danceteria offers eager audiences their first chance to hear the latest, most far-out bands.

Robin Holland

John Cage, of course, was also a furniture-music lover. With his "silent" piece *4'33"*, Cage took music out of the concert hall and into daily life in a more radical way than Muzak. With this piece, Cage suggests that music—any music: art, pop, pop experimental, or otherwise—is not needed, since all that is heard in those four minutes and thirty-three seconds is silences and naturally occurring sounds, and that is music enough. Here, it is not a question of mixing music into daily life. For Cage, life is music, in and of itself.

Somewhere between the extremes of Muzak and *4'33"* lies the work of Karlheinz Stockhausen. Stockhausen has created a vast range of music, with some of it environmental. In one instance, he designed a globe-shaped building lined with speakers for the performance of some of his electronic pieces at the 1970 Osaka World's Fair. Stockhausen also devised what Percy M. Young, in his article on the history of the concert in *The New Grove Dictionary of Music and Musicians* calls "continuous-event 'concerts' in non-specific buildings." Examples of these include *Ensemble* and *Musik für ein Haus,* during which the audience wanders among simultaneously performed, elaborately coordinated, yet random-sounding musical and music-theater "events." Then there is the 1972 *Alphabet für Liege,* actually an exhibition rather than a piece of music, that reveals the effects of acoustic vibrations on fish, dough, and the mental and physical capacities of people, among other things.

Max Neuhaus first toured with Stockhausen, then became the foremost environmental composer in the United States. Since 1970, Neuhaus' underwater whistles have serenaded swimmers, his electronic tones have helped plants grow in public greenhouses, and a grand organ chord mixed with street noises, has filtered out of a subway grating in Times Square. In the early 60s LaMonte Young, the minimalist innovator, created compositions not unlike Cage's *4'33"* but longer in duration, in which an audience was told that whatever happened in the next two hours was the beginning of a piece of music (these next two hours constituted the "music" itself). Young's colleagues at the time—all members of Fluxus, a loose-knit art/performance/music movement devoted to tearing down the boundaries between art and life—included the Japanese experimentalist Yoko Ono. who went on to play a dramatic role in the rock world as John Lennon's muse and wife.

No one ever thought that rock itself could be fused with environmental music. "This isn't background music, ever," Joe O'Brien of the New York City radio station WMCA told writer Bruce Jay Friedman in 1965. "It's there in the foreground. You don't put it on and have yourself a pleasant chitchat. You listen, participate. It's arrogant, aggressive, positive, slaps you right in the face. You listen or turn it off."

Yet the sound of rock 'n' roll has become so omnipresent that it actually is a large part of our environment of everyday sounds, and much of the time does serve as background music for chitchat. Just try to avoid the latest hit single. You could be freezing in some sort of shelter in the arctic zone and it wouldn't be long before a pipeline worker or an Inuit would come by with an insulated radio. Soon, you wouldn't be able to keep the latest tune out of your head. Indeed, we have gotten to the point where that latest hit is so drummed into our heads that the critic Walter Benjamin's famous question, "What form do you suppose a life would take that was determined at a decisive moment precisely by the street song last on everyone's lips?" is no longer rhetorical.

Today's pop experimentalists are beginning to use the music industry's methods of presentation and distribution that, for better or worse, keep our world filled with music. But their work along these lines is usually smarter and more thought-provoking than the strictly commercial stuff. For instance, Sire Records—one of the most adventurous rock labels—got into the spirit when it released *Portable Music,* a cassette featuring music by Talking Heads' David

Syndication International/Photo Trends

A d.j. plays records for employees in a biscuit factory at Osterley, in England.

Byrne and Jerry Harrison, as well as cuts by the Tom Tom Club, and aimed at Walkman users. And Philip Glass, at the invitation of WNET-TV in New York, devised a striking three-second musical I.D. for the station. Glass also wrote music for the torchlighting ceremony of the 1984 Los Angeles Olympics which reached millions, thanks to worldwide broadcast on TV, that great disseminator of music — undoubtedly pop experimental music's largest audience yet.

Even more stimulating to experimentalists, however, are the possibilities of the rock video form. Rock video was first conceived, not so much as a door to new musical perspectives, but as an entertaining hard sell, a fast-moving, decorative motif in discos and clubs, just something else to space out on. In fact, the early rock videos were just arty (and sometimes not so arty) commercials for new songs or albums. Sex and violence—almost always aimed towards women—figured prominently in these videos, as did visual clichés—such as trick editing, flash dissolves, slow motion, and cutaways. They quickly became as predictable and dull as the visual vocabulary of television commercials, which, of course, didn't make them any less popular. Indeed, by 1984, MTV—the main vehicle for rock video—was carried on 300 cable outlets, had nearly two thousand affiliates, and was snaking its tendrils into nearly 20 million homes across the United States.

Still, some pop experimentalists took to this new, though frequently abused, medium, and expanded its imaginative potential far beyond run-of-the-mill rock videos. For example, *Time* critic Jay Cocks praised director Josh White's video of the hit single "O Superman" by Laurie Anderson as "a satellite transmission from a forbidden planet." Her video of "Sharkey's Day" has an oddly simple, post-nuclear holocaust quality, with its juxtaposition of various low-tech types of computer animation—it is as if only these scraps of clunky technology have survived, and this is how we play with them. Talking Heads' "Burning Down the House" and "Once in a Lifetime" were touted as "psychedelic drawing room comedy." The dreamlike discontinuities that fill most rock videos are far too obvious. However, in Anderson's and Byrne's videos, the connections are more mysterious, and the effects more poetic. The viewer is encouraged to make his/her own connections between the images and the words and music of the song. The hope is that in doing so the viewer will reflect on the world in interesting new ways, even as he/she rushes to buy the record.

Despite their originality, pop experimentalists' rock videos still stick to the limited format demanded by a medium conceived for an audience with a short attention span. On the other hand, composer Robert Ashley's three-hour-long, seven-part video opera, *Perfect Lives,* directed by video artist John Sanborn, mixes music and imagery in more daring ways. Ashley started working in video long before the MTV mavens. Since the sixties, he has been involved in avant-garde multimedia performances. True to the esoteric spirit of such performances, *Perfect Lives,* with performers Ashley, pianist "Blue" Gene Tyranny, Jill Kroesen, and David Van Tieghem, is much less public than rock video. Visually and musically, it is too rich to be moving wallpaper for a rock club. It is also too verbal, with mazy narratives about several bland, mysteriously linked Midwestern lives, and meditations on perception and consciousness. It also includes a variety of music from pseudo-cocktail lounge piano tinkling (simulating the "high cocktail" style recorded in the 40s by Frankie Karl) to free rock improvisations and sumptuous, carefully interrelated visuals which require the audience to pay more attention than typical rock videos merit or can withstand. Ashley notes, however, that he does not mind if *Perfect Lives* does become just part of the audio-visual environment of someone's living room, playing on the VCR.

Ashley's opinion on how music should fit into daily life is far ahead of the MTV mentality. He feels that the deepest musical experiences do not occur in concert halls or discos, but in the privacy of the home, listening to music on records. "Pop music, and the pop music industry, is almost exclusively based on private experiences," says Ashley. "And the music most important to me—in our culture—is the music that I listen to by myself on records. I wanted to make serious music that had the quality of private experience." Ashley remarks that, just as when you listen to music at home you do not necessarily give it your full attention, so too with his video opera: "It's diametrically opposed to the idea of group viewing, but if you watch it with someone else, you have the freedom to talk to each other. You can also look at it for a minute or two and walk away and come back to it three months later." In fact, the narrative incoherence, free-association flow, and obscure content of *Perfect Lives* actually makes it hard for those uninitiated into the conventions and pre-suppositions of non-narrative forms to focus on the video for a long stretch of time. But in half-hour segments—the way Ashley feels it is most accessible—this unique opera is poignant, funny, and exalting. What's more, unlike rock videos, it is a visual/musical puzzle so cleverly put together that there is always something to go back to in each part that you did not catch the first time around. It is like watching a trippy soap opera (Ashley's use of the term "opera" has as much to do with soaps as it does with the Met) being broadcast from another planet somewhat like our own.

The new strides Ashley took are now directing other pop experimentalists. For instance, Peter Gordon, a one-time Ashley protege, is completing an extended/collaborative work with video artist Kit Fitzgerald, named after, and based on the table of contents of Thomas Hardy's novel *The Return of the Native.* This piece is as far removed from rock video pap as *Perfect Lives* is. Here, however, there are no words, and there is no dreamlike imagery. It is filled with placid, pastoral scenes intercut with outdoor performances by dancers Bill T. Jones and Arnie Zane, accompanied by a Gordon score for synthesizer that blends the energy of rock with the brooding quality of some twentieth century avant-garde music and—improbably but delightfully—the lilt of English country airs. No doubt other pop experimentalists will pursue this direction in video as well, especially now that listening to music at home on a stereo is giving way to a kind of "total" home entertainment: music you hear *and* see, on a TV set.

While television could be seen as the deformed offspring of cinema, in the case of rock video, the influence has worked in reverse. Movie-making has been affected by rock video—usually not the best of it—to the point that some of today's top-grossing box office hits, such as *Flashdance* and *Footloose,* are little more than extended rock videos. However, along with this trend, there have also been rock video-esque movies that, like *Perfect Lives* and the rock videos of David Byrne and Laurie Anderson, feature imagery and a pop experimentalist score far above the usual level of mindlessness. For example, Godfrey Reggio's *Koyaanisqatsi* which boasts a soundtrack by Philip Glass, strong visuals, and a complete absence of words. The effect is overpowering. Images and hypnotic music sweep you away; all emotional gestures are big ones; subtlety is missing—but then, subtlety is not the point. Instead, the point is to communicate ideas in the most direct way possible. In *Koyaanisqatsi* (the title is a Hopi word that means life out of balance), the ideas have to do with advanced technology and what it is doing to our environment today. The film, along with other musical films like Meredith Monk's haunting *Ellis Island*—a meditation on European immigrants to America in the early 1900s—is distinctly different from movies like *Flashdance.* However, in some ways they are not all *that* different, since nonverbal films with pop experimental scores have the same instant appeal that a movie like *Flashdance* does. It is clear why characters A, B, and C are doing whatever they are doing and what the events mean. There is not any sort of suspense as to what will happen next. All the viewer has to do is sit back and watch—and listen.

Like many films today, *Koyaanisqatsi*—as Robert Ashley's *Perfect Lives* may soon be—is available on video cassette for home viewing. But there is another way pop experimentalism takes music out of concert halls and blends it with daily life that is even more pervasive than rock video with ambient music. It was maverick rock musician Brian Eno who first had the idea of doing something interesting with this new type of canned music. He wanted to create a more sophisticated muzak—something like Satie and Milhaud's furniture music—that could be played, not only in public spaces, but at home, too, as an invisible but pleasing interior-design element.

In the mid-70s, Eno came up with the concept of ambient music—a music, as he notes, "intended to induce calm and a space to think. Ambient Music must be able to accommodate many levels of listening attention without enforcing one in particular," he continued. "It must be as ignorable as it is interesting." Eno tells a story of how, sick in bed in 1975, he discovered the appeal such music held. "My friend Judy Nylon visited me and brought me a record of eighteenth-century harp music. After she had gone, and [with] some considerable difficulty, I put on the record. Having laid down, I realized that the amplifier was set at an extremely low level, and that one channel of the stereo had failed completely. Since I hadn't the energy to get up and improve matters, the record played on almost inaudibly. This presented for me what was a new way of hearing music—as part of the ambience just as the color of the light and the sound of the rain were parts of that ambience."

The outlook recalls Cage's idea of the-whole-world-as-music. Indeed, Eno's musical roots have more in common with postwar avant-garde music than the rock scene in which he first captured attention. Like John Lennon and Peter Townshend, he started out as an art student,

This still from Meredith Monk's *Ellis Island* displays the video's nostalgic quality.

Bob Rosen

but turned to rock as a more direct way of communicating with an audience. En route to rock, though, he worked with English avant-garde composers such as Gavin Bryars and Cornelius Cardew, who both had initially been drawn to Cage's ideas about music.

Eno made his first splash in the 70s as the electronics/synthesizer man for the popular English rock group Roxy Music. In pirate drag and masked by elaborate makeup, he stood out onstage as much as lead singer Bryan Ferry did—to the high-powered Ferry's displeasure. Ultimately, Eno left the band, and has been active on his own ever since. His whirlwind history includes everything from starting Obscure, his own record label, to producing bands like Devo and Talking Heads, to collaborating with rockers David Bowie (the Eno touch is most evident on Bowie's *Low, Heroes,* and *Lodger*), Robert Fripp, and Phil Manzanera, to cutting albums of his own. His own albums became less and less rock-oriented over time, and *became* background music that could be intriguing if listened to carefully, but could be just as easily ignored. Here, too, Cage's influence is evident in the notion that listeners are free to pay attention or not, at will. But Eno's ambient music on *Music for Airports* and *On Land* is a lot easier to listen to than anything Cage ever wrote, for Eno limits himself to sounds that are, first and foremost, pleasing. As he himself admits, "I try to make pieces of music that are fun to listen to"—or fun not to listen to, if you are so inclined.

Eno was fascinated for years by the musical possibilities of tape recording, and composes his music, not at the piano or on score paper but in the recording studio. In doing so, he provides an input of various simple, tonal melodies, as well as synthesized sounds and sounds recorded from life, which are stored on a digital recall system. This material, in turn, is altered by means of a graphic equalizer. More recently, his ambient music albums feature fewer high-tech recording tricks. Still, the pieces all come out sounding more or less alike—slow-moving, soothing waves of sound, drones, sweet harmonies, thick sonic textures, and bits of pretty melodies that wash over the listener. The effect is tranquillizing, and sometimes melancholy. To sit and listen to ambient music, and "space out" may be just what is needed after a long, taxing day in the postmodern world—it's that undemanding. In fact, the music verges on non-music, a possibility of which Eno is aware. As he once remarked, "if you can do something that might just as well be nothing, but isn't, it is a much more powerful thing. But then, of course, you run the risk that it is nothing."

Nothing or not, Eno's own ambient music, as well as that of various collaborative projects, sells quite steadily and well. What's more, it has given rise to a whole new genre of pop experimental mood music from musicians such as the Swiss composer and electro-acoustic harpist Andreas Vollenweider, Los Angelean Harold Budd (who frequently collaborates with Eno), and the New Age composers—Deuter, Hans-Joachim Roedelius, and Kitaro, among them. All compose, essentially, pretty background music to "cool" out to, or—as Vollenweider puts it—music that "can move you to a point where you can liberate your imagination. You can create your own world on this carpet of music. But of course," he concludes, shifting gears just in time, "it's absolutely realistic, and not just a dream." Many composers of this music have adopted Eastern (particularly Zen or Tibetan Buddhist) religious beliefs, and many of their records are sold in incense-filled shops specializing in books on non-Western religion and philosophy as an aid to meditation.

Both rock video and ambient music, despite their success, have met with criticism, too. For example, some people find that rock video presents images that are too literal. Part of the pleasure of listening to rock music, they argue, is to shut your eyes and visualize whatever images come to mind. Rock video, on the other hand, does all the visualizing for the listener, making him or her more passive. Even the best rock videos are guilty of this accusation. Still, more adventurous works, like *Perfect Lives*, for example, feature such complex interlacings between music, words, and images that they escape this criticism. Indeed, listening to the music from Ashley's video opera without seeing the visuals is a less satisfying experience.

As for ambient music, many have dismissed it as pop experimentalism's answer to bubble gum. Yes, whether used for meditation or not, it does give the listener space to think, as its originator, Eno, intended. But ambient music is not so neutral that the listener can think whatever he or she wants to while listening to it. Its moods are very specific—and very limited, too, usually to either the sweetly sorrowful or the quietly enraptured.

For music presented in a new way that robs the listener of neither the freedom to visualize nor his or her own emotional range, turn to *Key*, the LP that constitutes Meredith Monk's extraordinary piece of "invisible theater." Monk, who has created numerous pieces of decidedly visible theater, here uses simple, haunting instrumentals, emotional but wordless singing, and some speaking to create, not merely a single mood, but a strong sense of evolving moods. Listening to it, it is as if one were at a play in which all the characters have vanished, with only the *feeling* of what they were doing and saying left behind and changing from scene to invisible scene. Perhaps more successful than any other pop experimentalist's efforts in this area, *Key* really does grant the listener freedom to make up his or her own stories as the music plays. However, because its emotions are so strongly expressed and varied, it stops thought from straying too quickly towards the ineffable.

Discography

Robert Ashley	PERFECT LIVES	*Lovely Music 4913 LMC 4947 (cassette only)*
Erik Satie	MUSIQUE D'AMEUBLEMENT, CINEMA ENTRACTE DE RELÂCHE	*Erato STU 71336*
Brian Eno	AMBIENT 1: MUSIC FOR AIRPORTS	*Editions EG*
Brian Eno	AMBIENT 4: ON LAND	*Editions EG*
Harold Budd/Brian Eno	THE PEARL	*Editions EG EGED 37*
Meredith Monk	KEY	*Lovely Music 1051*
Philip Glass	KOYAANISQATSI	*Antilles ASTA 1*

PERFOR- MANCE

The evening of November 21, 1976, was cool and cloudless in New York City, but the lobby of the Metropolitan Opera House pulsed with feverish energy. After receiving extremely enthusiastic reviews on its European tour, Philip Glass and Robert Wilson's four-and-a-half-hour-long opera, *Einstein on the Beach,* was about to have its American premiere. If composer and director were strictly avant-garde types, the crowd gathered that memorable evening was anything but low-rent. Yes, there were struggling musicians, dancers, poets, and artists. But the city's *haute monde* were also present: world-famous rock and classical musicians, painters, novelists, poets, designers, theater artists, and architects, as well as rich patrons and their fashionable coteries. The members of the crowd were diverse, but all of them shared one thought: something unprecedented was about to happen. They were not to be disappointed.

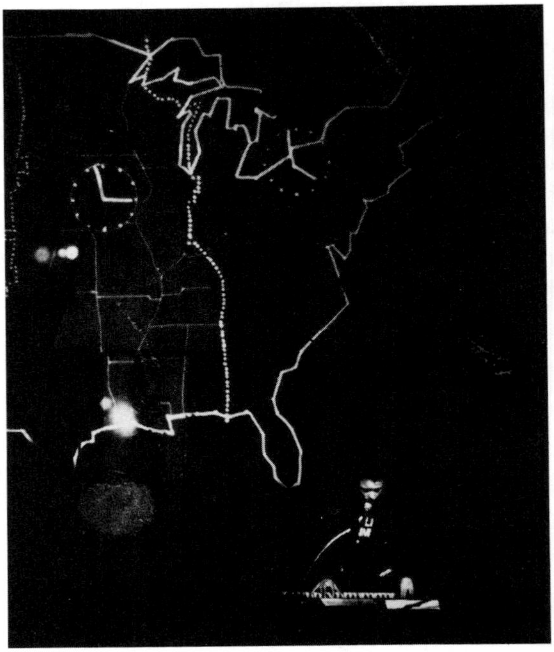
Paula Court

Laurie Anderson, performing *United States 1-4* generates multiple meanings by blending music, lyrics, and slide projections, such as this of a "personals" ad.

People filed in, and soon all the seats in the vast opera house were filled. Downstage left, before a gray drop curtain, sat two women. One was white, the other black, and both were dressed in the Einstein manner: a man's white short-sleeve shirt, baggy pants, suspenders, and sneakers. They both had a frozen attitude, and were murmuring to themselves. The black woman, Sheryl Sutton, was a longtime member of Robert Wilson's theater troupe, the Byrd Hoffman School of Byrds, which owed its odd name to a teacher Wilson had had as a child. The white woman was choreographer Lucinda Childs, known for her austere, lucidly structured dance pieces. From the orchestra pit—not filled with the Met's orchestra now, but with the Philip Glass Ensemble—an electric organ intoned three long-held, descending notes. The sense of expectation in the crowd mounted.

Gradually, the audience grew still and the house lights dimmed. In the darkness, a soft chant of numbers began, sweet and light, accompanied by the organ. Minutes passed, then, suddenly, the drop curtain flew up. The Glass Ensemble burst into a hard-driving, high-decibel whirl of sound. From the top of a tall erector-set tower, a boy hurled paper missiles. Childs performed a strange, twitchy walking-dance. Before a gray backdrop, in eerie, smoky light, a locomotive chugged slowly across the spacious stage. And that is how one of the most supercharged evenings in the history of twentieth-century musical theater began.

What is "supercharged" musical theater? How can it be performed in an opera house? What kind of musical theater is it? Like *Fiddler on the Roof? Einstein on the Beach* is not like any opera or musical comedy ever seen before. First, there is no plot—just elaborate, surrealistic stage images, constructed on a grand scale, and linked, not logically, but in free-associative order. Nor are there characters, but just a lot of people dressed more or less like Einstein. There are no songs, either. The music is continuous, and the only lyrics are numbers and the solfeggio syllables one hears in that old favorite from *The Sound of Music,* "Doe a Deer": 1-2-3-4-5-6-7-8, 1,1-2,2-2,3-2,4-2, or la-fa-la-si-do-si, and so on, numbers and syllables that express the rhythmic and melodic structure of the music.

This music was not unlike what Glass fans had grown used to since the early 70s. This time, though, the harmonies were richer, almost romantic-sounding. (Glass himself cited the nineteenth-century French composer Hector Berlioz as an inspiration). Those lucky enough to have seen Robert Wilson's earlier, mostly silent "operas" (among them the 12-hour-long *The Life and Times of Joseph Stalin*) were not wholly shocked, either. But while Wilson's earlier works were colorful, homemade-looking, and performed mainly by non-professionals, *Einstein on the Beach* was quick-tempoed, coolly gray and white, slick, and snappy—a multimillion dollar, avant-garde, glamour extravaganza with a cast of pros.

The opera had as much to do with the century's greatest physicist as *Stalin* had to do with one of its cruellest dictators—not much, in any obvious sense. Rather, the stage images and mathematically precise music conjured up the spirit of Einstein, of his physics with its daring speculations about space and time—and the spirit of the Nuclear Age. To emphasize the theme yet again, a violinist, also dressed like the music-loving physicist, unkempt mop of silver hair and all, sat on the upstage edge of the pit in prominent view, sawing furiously on his violin.

Hours passed. People watched, or chatted, or strolled around to visit friends. But surrounded by the repetitive music and nearly static stage action, most grew mesmerized by the slow, flowing phenomenon of time itself, echoed in the music and stage images. As poet David Shapiro writes, "They remind me of time Albert said/Always going but never gone."

The emotional effect of all of this was intense. Still, most members of the audience could not easily articulate why this was so. Though Glass' ensemble played as loudly as the most-deafening rock bands, the mood in the Met that night was not like that of a rock concert. No one got up and boogied, nor was there the direct, electric contact between performers and audience that makes rock concerts so thrilling. *Einstein on the Beach* was cooler than a rock concert, more detached, but it generated its own electricity. Take for example, a section from Act Two. One of the longest scenes, it is set in a place that was half-courtroom, complete with judge and jury, and half-jail, complete with two prisoners—a weird setting, but not moving in and of itself. The jury, making tiny gestures with their fingers as if they are writing on invisible blackboards, softly sing numbers to a quick, lilting organ accompaniment—a chant consisting of only two alternating notes, yet somehow tremendously exhilirating. At the same time, Lucinda Childs, in a chic white frock, wanders around and then lays down on a big white bed in the center of the courtroom talking quietly and evenly about being in a supermarket and how she had been avoiding the beach. The anecdote, which she keeps repeating, sounds pointless, then boring, then bonkers, then funny, then sad—these many emotions created without the words or Childs' tone changing. Something about the blend of elements gives the scene a powerfully poignant, poetic quality. The music is as smooth and steady as a drive down an

Philip Glass and Robert Wilson's *Einstein on the Beach* featured hypnotic music and haunting stage imagery.

Johan Elbers

interstate highway early on a sunny weekday morning; the numbers sung are so logical, the courtroom is so orderly (though no one knows what is on trial), and the ominous jail, which contradicts the subdued yet carefree music, gives the audience a sense of imprisonment and freedom at the same time. This potent, hard-to-convey poetry, not spelled out to the audience, but something the viewer must put together on his own, made *Einstein on the Beach* the phenomenal success it was.

In time, the opera neared its end. The climax—set in a gigantic spaceship with lights flashing wildly in time with ear-splitting, swift-moving amplified keyboards and wind instruments, and the chorus chanting more numbers at crazily high speeds—brought down the house. The closing moments were quiet, though, almost offhand. The music ended; the lights went up; the audience roared; ovation followed standing ovation. *Einstein on the Beach* had triumphed; history had been made.

Despite two sold-out performances and ecstatic reviews, all involved did not rise to meteoric fame—at least, not right away. Wilson ended up deeply in debt, and several weeks later Glass was driving a cab. But the stage had been set for a new kind of musical theater—visually enthralling, musically simple yet evocative, spiritually elevating—that provided an impetus for the works being created by pop experimentalists today.

Of course, *Einstein on the Beach* was not a "first" in every sense of the word. The history of similarly adventurous musical theater in the late nineteenth and twentieth centuries is a rich one. It ranges from the Wagnerian "total artwork"—mystical operas that united all the arts—to the anti-art antics of Italian Futurists; from the "theater of cruelty" envisioned by the French director and writer Antonin Artaud, to the "poor theater" of Jerzy Grotowski; from

Guitar-smashing enhanced the charismatic appeal of some of the more theatrical rock groups.

Chris Walter/Retna Ltd.

the epic theater originated by Bertolt Brecht and contributed to by composers Kurt Weill (who collaborated with Brecht on *The Threepenny Opera*), Paul Dessau, and Hanns Eisler, to the ritualistic stage spectacles of composer Carl Orff; from the madcap "Happenings" of the 60s to the performance art that first surfaced in the 70s and continues to this day.

While varied, the types of experimental theater in which music plays a main role share certain features that recur in theater works by pop experimentalists today. For instance, all break the rules of psychological realism, and reject realism's emphasis on believable characters and plots. These experimentalists strive for a stylized theater instead. Sometimes their stylizations distance the viewer from the stage action, so that he or she can judge the action more rationally, which is harder for the viewer to do if he or she is caught up in them. At other times, the stylization has a more irrational quality that lifts viewers up to a spiritual realm high above that of daily life.

In both cases, music is a key factor in the stylization. Sometimes—in Brecht's epic theater, for example—music helps the audience stay aloof from the action by cutting into the characters' stories with sung commentary. At other times—in Robert Wilson's marathon operas, for example—music entrances the audience, as does the snail-paced, dreamy stage imagery.

Both modes of theatrical stylization go against the conventions of realistic Western theater, and are inspired by traditions outside it. They draw on many different kinds of theater, from puppet shows and street theater to Japanese Nō plays and Indonesian shadow plays. In turning to traditions out of the mainstream, the creators of these stylized plays and stage pieces make an implicit (or sometimes explicit) protest, not only against Western theater, but against the Western world's status quo. By doing so, they hope to suggest to the audience ways to change that status quo, or at least to see through it, by pushing perception past the limits it prescribes.

While way-out experimental theater was mainly for intellectuals in the 60s, rockers came up with compelling theatrical gimmicks of their own. They made some serious attempts to harness rock's unruly energies to forge a new kind of musical theater. In fact, rock concerts were becoming more like high-energy multimedia rituals than anything the word concert had ever suggested. They included the total environments created during the psychedelia rage, with flashing lights and protoplasmic blobs simulating the LSD experience. But also, on the stage itself, the play was becoming the thing. The performers were no longer content to shake their shaggy heads and leave it at that. The sonic flamboyance and emotional excess of the era had its visual side, too.

"I could hear the notes in my head," said Pete Townshend of the Who, "but I couldn't play them on the guitar... It used to frustrate me incredibly. I used to try to make up visually for what I couldn't play as a musician ... It became a huge visual thing. In fact I forgot all about the guitar because my visual thing was more my music than the actual guitar... I banged it; I let if feed back and ... rubbed it up against the microphone, did anything. It didn't deserve any credit or any respect. I used to bang it and hit it against walls and throw it on the floor. And one day it broke." A rash of highly theatrical, if somewhat gratuitous instrument-abuse rituals ensued. Guitars were not the only targets: Keith Emerson (of Emerson, Lake and Palmer) would send his Hammond organ flying on its wheels, ride it like a bronco, and knife the keyboard to hold down the notes.

Gradually, these hysterical theatrics became more and more like theater. David Bowie created a series of stage personae with startling makeup and weirdly stylized behavior, and used stage sets that looked like exquisite dioramas. Heavy metal developed its cult-of-the-devil scenarios along the lines of Alice Cooper, a made-up stage persona (a *Cincinnati Enquirer* headline told the real story: "Beneath Horror Makeup, He's a Golf Freak") who tortured audiences with kitschy devil's heads, stuck on medieval parapets, hissing purple smoke, entrances on giant brass beds lowered from the ceiling, and film projections of him stalking through graveyards. Other groups limited themselves to giant light shows or hydraulic lifts.

By the 70s, the idea of the rock concert as theater had become so implicit that it was hard to look at even a bare rock stage with four musicians and not notice its theatrical aspect. "I would go to a play in the early evening," says playwright-turned-composer Glenn Branca, "and then to a rock concert at night. The play was what I loved and what I was interested in, but the rock concert was so exciting. And of course, someone who was coming from the theater would easily see the theater in a rock concert because you're dealing with the same elements entirely. I had always envisioned my theater in a rock context."

Before the 60s ended, there were fully shaped works of rock music theater as well. *Hair* and *Jesus Christ Superstar* played Broadway and spawned world-touring companies and movies. The Who's *Tommy* blasted 40,000 watts of amplification through opera houses in Copenhagen, New York, Hamburg, Berlin, and Munich. It was billed as a rock opera, with cohesive, three-part structure, an overture (called an underture), and leitmotifs like the "see me, feel me, touch me, heal me" motif that the title character comes back to at important points in his development.

Tommy is a horribly abused deaf, dumb, and blind boy who rises to become a cult preacher of "the way," a pinball wizard, and a rock star. Teaching his disciples the road to enlightenment at a summer camp, he makes them practice pinball while wearing dark sunglasses and earplugs. They rebel, and the end of the opera is one long, unified work that repeats themes related to Tommy's self-realization. But despite *Tommy's* classical structure, the Who kept the rock drive going throughout. As writer Albert Goldman put it, they "worked the Met like a grind-house in Liverpool."

All these exciting precedents notwithstanding, by the mid-70s a new musical theater that mixed the gutsy appeal of rock with the intelligence of avant-garde theater had still not materialized. Funding was scarce. Producers did not want to take chances with something too risky. Pop experimental music had allure, but the lack of plot, characters, and clear-cut messages in pop experimental musical theater caught people off guard. And, at least in the 70s, people like Glass, Wilson, and Meredith Monk were not ready to make the kind of compromises that would bring angels fluttering down en masse, checkbooks in hand, and ensure them a good box-office following. And so money for experimental musical theater came mainly from grants and private patrons. Performances took place outside mainstream rock venues, and outside mainstream theatrical ones, too. Because of this, the works reached a rather limited audience.

Then, there was the problem of the word opera, which leading pop experimenters applied to their pieces. It put people off, especially pop-oriented younger fans. Apart from *Tommy* and *Hair,* people liked their rock performed at concerts, at clubs, or—maybe best of all—at home on their stereos. Opera meant *Don Giovanni, La Traviata, Lohengrin, Der Rosenkavalier,* and getting dressed up and sitting in a big, formal theater, bored to tears. Operas had a dusty, museum-piece air about them. You went to one—if you went at all—and dozed, or you walked out.

In fact, when Robert Wilson called his mega-productions operas, he was not thinking of Verdi or Mozart, but more of the maverick American experimental writer Gertrude Stein. By the 1920s, Stein was writing unprecedented, nonsensical verbal melanges that lacked plot, characters, stage directions, or indications of who said what. These texts were meant to be staged as static theatrical landscapes in which nothing happened. Audiences, Stein hoped, would not pay attention to the story (there was none), but to the passing of time and the way it was marked by her rhythmic, repetitive, but contentless phrases. Watching such an opera was more like cloud-gazing than like waiting to see what would happen to Rigoletto next. Unfortunately, few composers cottoned to Stein's quirky ideas. Virgil Thomson was the most notable exception, though, with his marvelous, tuneful opera *Four Saints in Three Acts,* based on a Stein text.

Wilson's own operas were even more bizarre than *Four Saints.* Though often performed on proscenium stages like any ordinary opera, Wilson's productions lasted a lot longer and often included complete silence for hours on end. During performances, people were free to come and go as they pleased. They could fall asleep; they could talk; or they could sit and watch the elaborate, ever-shifting stage imagery and various areas of stage action. That action and imagery had a dream-like feel; indeed, the scenes were almost live enactments of Wilson's own private dreams, though, as critic Leo Bersani notes, "the anonymity of Wilson's theater makes it universally accessible."

So, while music critics bewailed the lack of new experimental operas and successful rock operas, Wilson kept coming up with operas of his own. What's more, he gave that off-putting term a surprising new appeal. With *Einstein on the Beach,* which received far more press coverage than Wilson's earlier efforts, people began talking about a new kind of opera, one that was charged with the energy that made rock performances so potent, and would draw larger, more diverse audiences.

One particular opera house provided a focal point. The Brooklyn Academy of Music, founded in 1861 when Brooklyn was one of the nation's largest cities and had one of the largest opera-going populations, had come upon hard times with the decline of its surrounding neighborhood in the 50s and 60s. In 1967, a native Brooklynite and ex-dancer Harvey Lichtenstein took over as executive director and soon "the darkened stage was illuminated by light glancing off . . . large helium-filled pillows . . . electronic music assaulted the ears from all sides . . . with decor by Andy Warhol," as noted by *Newsweek.* Lichtenstein made the Academy a center of innovative dance, and was beginning to lure audiences from outside the borough by presenting programs that were too risky for Manhattan halls of comparable size to stage. The Academy soon became a mecca for experimentation in all performing arts. Besides dance, the controversial works of the Living Theater and of Jerzy Grotowski were performed on the large stage of the Opera House, followed by Robert Wilson's early pieces. It was natural that the Academy would become the foremost exponent of the new opera. By the late 70s, Lichtenstein felt, "minimalist music had come of age . . . the maturity of the work, the existence of large-scale pieces, and the existence of a supportive audience hit us, and we decided to promote it with a festival." The "Next Wave" festival, as it is called, began its first season with Philip Glass' second opera, *Satyagraha* (hailed by *Newsweek* as "that rare thing—a thoughtful new opera that succeeds"), and has grown with a roster of operas, multimedia events, and large-ensemble music pieces by Laurie Anderson, Steve Reich, Peter Gordon, Glenn Branca, and many others. Recent music-theater works have included, not only *The Games,* by Meredith Monk and Ping Chong and a revival of *Einstein on the Beach,* but also Lee Breuer's *The Gospel at Collonus,* a work with music by Bob Tilson with the Five Blind Boys of Alabama. The festival encourages collaborations between like-minded composers and directors—they're helping to put the Los Angeles composer John Adams together with director Peter Sellars at the moment, for example—and the Academy does a lot of what Lichtenstein calls "missionary work," subsidizing tours, creating television interest, and providing hu-

Robert Wilson's hallucinatory stage tableaux set the pace for pop experimental musical theater.

Jennifer Kotter

manities programs for colleges and public forums. "It's still a push, but it's a helluva lot easier than it was five years ago," says Lichtenstein. It's gotten to the point, in fact, where rock stars such as David Bowie and Andy Summers (of the Police) are coming to the festival, wanting to do experimental work themselves.

Philip Glass' *Satyagraha* suggests one direction in which opera may be headed. Though later presented at BAM, it was first commissioned by the city of Rotterdam, Netherlands, at a time when the composer's work had still failed to impress America's musical establishment. It is scored for operatic voices and a conventional orchestra rather than for Glass' ensemble, and deals with the early days of M.K. Gandhi's political career in South Africa, where he developed the concept of satyagraha, or non-violence. The opera is softer and more lulling than *Einstein on the Beach*. Sung in Sanskrit, the libretto—which Glass wrote in collaboration with writer Constance De Jong—featured snippets from the *Bhagavad Gita,* an episode in the Indian religious epic Mahabharata from which Gandhi gained great inspiration throughout his life. The words of the opera, however, did not follow the action, but commented on it. The action itself consisted of Wilsonesque tableaux, each one portraying an episode in Gandhi's life in South Africa.

Though basically plotless, *Satyagraha* does have a certain forward movement. More significantly, it has a clearer meaning than *Einstein on the Beach,* and one particularly appropriate to this time when the political climate in America has become so conservative. Children of the 60s, Glass and De Jong still harbored hopes for further political and social change. With this opera, they held Gandhi up as a possible role model for such change today. Indeed, Glass has noted, "his life's aims were achieved, wielding the weapons of satyagraha . . . combined with the force of his personality alone is, for me, Gandhi's message for our time." The opera has a quiet, contemplative feeling, one that almost makes you believe that it does not really matter if such change occurs at all. Yet, its message that change can occur through nonviolent means comes across.

With *Satyagraha,* Glass' career took a decisive turn. Earlier, he had written theater music for the group, The Mabou Mines. In fact, Joanne Akalaitis, one of that group's prime movers, had been Glass' wife, and is mother of their two children. But the Mabou Mines pieces were modestly scaled. Now works of larger scope—true operas—occupied the composer's time and creativity. With the success of his first two operas, lucrative commissions poured in and the presentation of newer ones in America seemed guaranteed.

Indeed, Glass' third opera, *Akhnaten,* which premiered in Stuttgart, Germany, opened at both the Houston Opera and the New York City Opera late in 1984. Along with *Satyagraha,* it is now part of the City Opera's repertory. Both also continue to be performed in European opera houses, where they are received enthusiastically.

Akhnaten offers a somewhat more clear-cut plot than *Satyagraha*. It recounts the rise and fall of an Egyptian ruler considered to be the first monotheist. Key moments of his reign comprise most of the opera, which, nevertheless, is far from action-packed. Rather, each scene is played out as a static tableau, the mood of which—whether festive, melancholy, bellicose, pensive, or eerie—is evoked by the music. Sung primarily in Egyptian, Hebrew, and Akkadian (with English narration), the words do not illuminate the story as much as lend it an air of intense exoticism. But it is the music, most of all, that creates this mysterious atmosphere, whether in the orgiastic funeral in Act One, with its unpredictable syncopations, and barking and shrill vocal lines going on simultaneously, accompanied by relentlessly pounding drums; or in the haunting, lyrical duet between Akhnaten and Nefertiti, his wife and queen—he is a counter-tenor, and she is a mezzo soprano who often sings lower than he does—or in the mournful, tender, wordless song that Akhnaten and his daughters sing, as the king becomes more and more cut off from his subjects. Indeed, the historical figure, Akhnaten, remains an unsolved riddle throughout the opera. Sigmund Freud suggested that he may have been a founder of Judaism, while the archaeologist Immanuel Veilkovsky thought he may have been the historical Oedipus, and sired a daughter with his mother. Conjunctions between ancient Egypt, Judaism, Freud, the Oedipus complex, incest, and the history of the Arabs, the Jews, and psychoanalysis in the twentieth century offer dizzying perspectives to those who care to inspect them; Glass does not. He simply presents a musical question mark, and lets us make of it what we will. His opera is essentially a meditative spectacle, with music that takes us into a vanished world we can never truly know—though one which, in the course of listening to the opera, we may ponder. The repetitiveness and slight variations in the music—still present in the opera, though to a lesser degree than in Glass' earlier music—lure the listener into a state of speculation. Indeed, that is what makes *Akhnaten* so strangely compelling; it sounds as enigmatic as its subject.

Today, Glass' operas—at the forefront of pop experimental musical theater—are warmly received by the institutions that once ignored his music. One can well imagine his feeling of triumph, for after years of put-downs, he is now in great demand—not only because he fits into the slot of contemporary opera composer that many companies feel obliged to fill, but because performances of his operas keep selling out.

With his upcoming operas, Glass reaches out to even broader audiences, those that shy away from any book, film, or stage piece that lacks a narrative. It is true that the composer himself was once a sworn enemy of narrative theater. "It's telling a story about our lives and the way our daily life is a story," he complained. This, he said, "simply was boring, it was shitty . . . What we wanted . . . was an experience that seemed to be more in tune with our real perceptions. . . . We've moved so far away from being satisfied . . . with narrative models . . . that perhaps the extremism of our time has to do with trying to find an experience which goes . . . right beyond the everyday world that we see." In 1984, working once more with Robert Wilson on the massive opera *the CIVIL warS,* for some sections of which he composed music, Glass adhered to that anti-narrative bias. (David Byrne of Talking Heads also wrote music for parts of *the CIVIL warS.* These sections were performed at the Walker Art Center in Minneapolis. The whole production, intended to last half a day, was scheduled to play in Los Angeles during the 1984 Olympics. Funding fell through, however, and performances were cancelled. Now, there is talk of staging portions of the piece in 1985 or '86.)

Glass' most recent operas, however, feature straight-ahead stories. *The Juniper Tree,* based on a Grimm's fairy tale and composed in collaboration with Robert Moran, will have clear dramatic conflicts, characters, and a plot. Instead of hypnotizing audiences with musical repetitions, Glass says he will use them to express a character's emotions. Those emotions may seem less ambiguous than real-life emotions, but that does not bother Glass at all.

Another forthcoming opera, based on Doris Lessing's space fiction novel *The Making of the Representative from Planet 8* will also deal with emotions in a simplified way. This time, though, it will not be the emotions of individual characters, but of an entire imaginary civilization that inhabits another, earth-like planet faced with the prospect of total extinction. Glass and Lessing see this grim situation as analogous to our own. To get that idea across, the composer will once again use his simple music, not to entrance an audience, but to express clear, easily grasped feelings.

By writing operas that express such feelings, Glass has moved in a direction few of his early admirers could have anticipated. Until the mid-70s, his music was impassioned, yet also

The early years of Gandhi's political career take on an otherworldly air in Glass' *Satyagraha*.

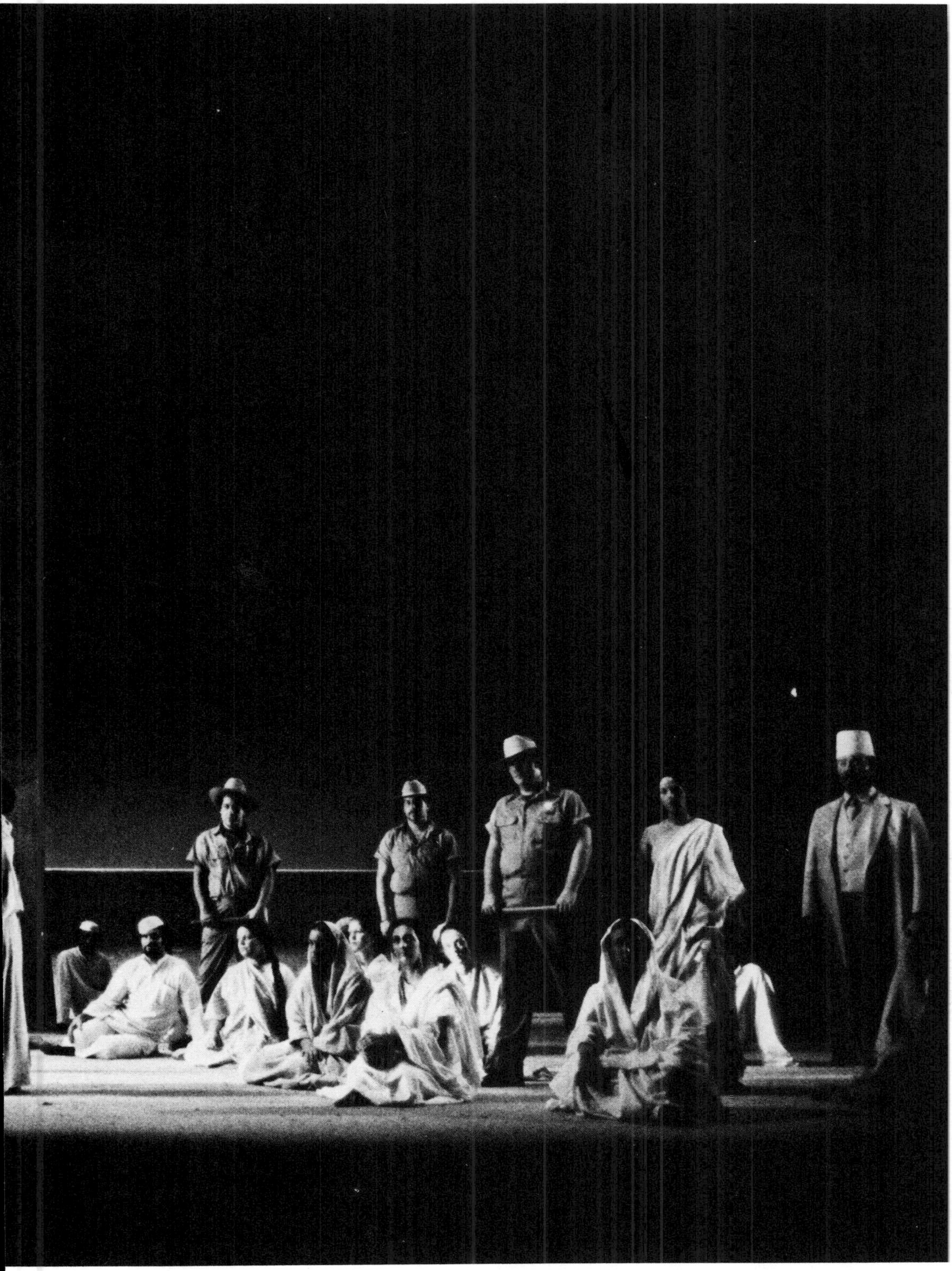

Johan Elbers

Beatriz Schiller

The Games, by Meredith Monk (at left) and Ping Chong, includes several post-apocalyptic stunts.

quite mechanical-sounding (indeed, Glass himself often likened his music to a "space machine"). Traditional operas, on the other hand, required symphonic orchestras and flesh-and-blood human characters rather than robots. With this in mind, and wishing, too, to work within the prescribed perimeters of opera companies, Glass now scores his operas for an orchestra and operatically trained voices, and the music is more emotionally illustrative than in his earlier pieces. Tempo and dynamics shift with a scene's mood. Fewer repetitions and more sonorities of unamplified orchestral instruments gives the music a traditional quality.

Not everyone appreciates Glass' current operatic music, and some critics are especially censorius. But, as Glass noted in a recent interview, "At this point in my work, I know what I want to do. As long as producers want to produce the works and audiences want to buy tickets, who cares about the critics?" At present, among several other projects Glass is composing a new work for his ensemble, which will accompany a dance piece by choreographer David Gordon. It will be interesting to see if and how Glass will bring the warmer, more varied quality of his operatic scores to this new composition.

Unlike Philip Glass' operas, Meredith Monk's multimedia musical theater pieces of the 70s were less cool and detached. *Vessel, Education of a Girlchild,* and *Quarry* all boasted strong emotional qualities, and had a plain, lumpy, less pristine look and sound than Glass' works. This was especially true of *Quarry,* with its homey but somehow drab, simultaneously presented domestic scenes. It had an autobiographical flavor that distinguished it sharply from *Einstein on the Beach.*

Indeed, most of Monk's musical theater pieces of the 70s seemed autobiographical—not explicitly, but in a more spiritual sense. In fact, her lifestyle and past are not especially out of the ordinary. When she first started living in New York City in the mid-60s, she performed her own experimental dance pieces, and established a reputation as a choreographer. In time, she branched out into other performing fields as well. Soon, her dance pieces blossomed into mixed-media events for which she wrote the music, devised blocking and choreography, and designed the sets. She also performed in these pieces, along with her own predominantly female troupe of players, known collectively as The House.

Her versatility and innovation were evident in the unusual and indigenous environments in which Monk staged her musical theater pieces—industrial lofts, streets, museums, and school gymnasiums. At times, the audience was actually transported from one locale to another during the piece.

Uncustomary playing spaces required both performers and audience to move around; a format of a fragmentary, often nonverbal series of sketches, like fairy tale episodes; the archetypal figures (kings, saints, girl children, old women, soldiers) presented in those sketches—all features gave Monk's operas the qualities of a mythical journeys. They were not outer journeys, though, but inner ones, perhaps towards greater self-understanding or towards a more perfect understanding between people.

Like Glass' operas, Monk's have little story line, and words do not play an important part. And Monk's music is not unlike Glass' in its repetitiveness, though it has a warmer, more human quality, especially her vocal music, the effect of which ranges from heartrending to hilarious. But Monk's messages, unlike those conveyed in Glass' operas, are homey and not at all grandiose—though not always easy to decipher. Often there are feminist overtones, and a communal attitude that seems a welcome alternative to the stylized scenes of modern-day horror and dehumanization that her pieces often portray.

Meredith Monk's most recent musical theater piece, *The Games,* created in collaboration with theater artist Ping Chong and first performed in 1983 at the Schaubühne theater in

West Berlin and, as mentioned, at The Brooklyn Academy of Music in 1984, is perhaps her least personal work to date. It once again deals with the issue many artists see as the most important one the world faces today—the possibility of nuclear war. "I think *The Games* is a very political piece," Monk notes. "During the Berlin rehearsals there were reports that the Americans were planning mass gravesites in Europe, and then American missiles were deployed in Germany. The piece was made as we were considering the possibility of the end of the world. It's about trying to make sense of a civilization that is disintegrating."

The "sense" Monk and Ping Chong make of civilization is at times a bit simplistic. Scenically stunning and colorfully lit, *The Games* offers a worldview that assures us that someday, somehow, all contradictions will be resolved. Presented as a series of choreographed and increasingly creepy games played out in a post-nuclear holocaust, spaceshiplike arena, the piece tends to illuminate life in rather syrupy hues. The central message is that if only we rid ourselves of the aggressions and fears that led us to build nuclear arms, the world will be a better place and people will be happier. The idea seems, unfortunately, a big, optimistic, naive "if only." Still, Monk's music (scored mainly for voices, electronic keyboards, and at one point, bagpipes), with its intimate, direct quality, often brings the sweeping statements about civilization today, found in *The Games,* down to a more personal, emotional level.

Monk, who came of age in the 60s, seems to retain the faith in communality and peace-through-mutual-understanding that rockers sang about in the halcyon era. This faith is certainly needed—now more than ever—but when Monk and Ping Chong apply it to the destiny of the human race it comes out sounding pat. Paradoxically, Monk's theater music has been used more effectively by Vienna's Serapions Theater, whose surrealistic $\frac{\sqrt{PATT}}{\mathcal{V}=\sqrt{2g\cdot h}<?}$ features lush stage imagery, devoid of any paraphraseable message, but as emotionally rich as the music itself.

As radical as Glass' and Monk's pop experimental operas seem, they are actually quite politically neutral. This is true of *Satyagraha,* which is more a solemn meditation on Gandhi than a call to action. And it is true of *The Games,* which is more elegaic in mood. As Charles Newman notes in his long essay "The Post-Modern Aura," "It cannot be emphasized enough that the Avant-Garde was for Europe a profoundly cultural and political revolution, while for America, from the very first, it was essentially an *aesthetic* movement—a technical reform of syntax, vocabulary, and tone—and so it remains." In light of this, it is not surprising that these operas, like pop experimental music as a whole, try to raise the audience to a higher level of consciousness or present a simple, easy-to-follow picture of the world, rather than to attempt something more complex or thought-provoking.

On the other hand, the opera *Birth of a Poet,* which premiered in Rotterdam and will, one hopes, eventually be performed in the United States, is boldly political—maybe too political for cultural groups who will support pop experimentalists only if they stick to spiritual matters, and leave politics alone. Peter Gordon composed the music, novelist Kathy Acker wrote the historically wide-ranging and sexually graphic libretto, artist David Salle did the sets, and famed avant-gardiste Richard Foreman directed the opera. Unlike most pop experimental music theater pieces, *Birth of a Poet* boasts a complex theme—the relationship between language and politics—and is set in a doomed, gritty, futuristic utopia with expressionistic overtones, in Augustan Rome, and in present-day Iran. This opera is not lulling, nor is the music. Numerous musical textures, including jarring noise rock, machine-music, and exotic scoring for harps and solo voice, are juxtaposed in a sonic collage that challenges listeners far more than most experimental theater music.

Whether politically provocative or poetic, the operas discussed so far are very different from *Rigoletto.* Musically they are as compelling as the best rock, and visually they are far more intriguingly staged than traditional operas. Nevertheless, they stay within certain operatic perimeters, especially in the use of the proscenium stage, with its see-through "fourth wall" between audience and performers.

On the other hand, Laurie Anderson's pieces—she calls them "a kind of opera"—offer a more direct interaction between performer and audience. Her earliest efforts were low-budget affairs that advanced phenomenological ideas in a breezy manner. For instance, she played her violin on a street for whoever passed by while wearing ice skates embedded in a block of ice, and fiddled until the ice melted. Or, she created conceptual art installations in which the printed word, the photographic image, the art object, and recorded music (basically simple songs she composed herself) were all blended to play off one another, and set off chains of association in the viewer/listener's mind. By the late 70s, Anderson herself began to play a more central role in her works, and the emphasis switched from installation to live performance. Her performance pieces grew more complex, incorporating slides, films, synthesizers, and instruments of Anderson's own invention. These pieces were eventually anthologized into *United States, Parts 1-4.*

The two-evening, eight-hour-long *United States, Parts 1-4* (which includes "O Superman," a hit single in England that sold 150,000 copies worldwide, and launched Anderson's career as a new music star) is like a stand-up comic's routine. However, it is done in a more sophisticated manner, and on a far more spectacular scale, replete with slide show, vivid lighting effects and, of course, Anderson's half-sung, half-spoken songs accompanied by an array of musical instruments and technological gadgetry.

In some ways, Anderson's musical theater pieces resemble those of Monk and Glass. They are plotless and characterless, and built up from short vignettes with connections that are more poetic than logical. (Anderson's book *United States* gives a good sense of how these connections work, with stills from the piece arranged in the same sequence as the various parts of the performance.) There is no drama in *United States, Parts 1-4,* and no suspense. The center of attention is Laurie Anderson herself, a pert, gamine-type with a dry, deadpan delivery. Dressed in mannish attire, all black or white except for bright socks, and sporting a short, spiky punk hairdo, she comes on as a kind of New Wave raconteur/musician. She cradles her white violin in her arm, and plays it with a Darth Vadar-esque neon bow or her invented tape-bow—made from prerecorded tapes—that lets out a babble of words when she passes it over a tape head on the violin bridge.

United States, Parts 1-4 is more like a performed journal than a traditional opera, with mini-stories and observations of daily life (though devoid of a journal's introspective and confessional passages). It seeks to hold the audience's attention with its mood, its display of cleverly manipulated electronic gizmos, its well-told tales, and its shifts from pensive to more upbeat tempos, rather than with suspenseful plot twists and character interactions.

Still, despite the shifts and gizmos, the mood of the work stays the same throughout: a mood that captures the beauty, poignance, and desolation of America's great, cold distances, distances spanned by merciless, omnipotent technology and ruled by the somehow sinister corporate interests behind it. Laurie Anderson's United States is home for no one. Like the big, bare stage on which the work of the same name is performed, it is chilly, comfortless, and easy to get lost in, colored like a black-and-silvery-white image on a TV set, in which the hues of numerals on digital clocks and CRT screens occasionally glimmer. Contemplating this America brings on a certain sadness, a sense of disenchantment. It could have been a home

Both the music and the graphics of Anderson's *United States 1-4* are at once naive and sophisticated.

Jennifer Kotter

for us, one whispers ruefully—but then, was it *ever* possible for anyone but American Indians to feel at home here?

This sense of disenchantment comes through in many ways. It is in Anderson's cool, white, well-educated, wry voice, that lends a chill significance to even the most nondescript line (she certainly isn't Joan Rivers). It is in her careful, calculated body movements, from which spontaneity and joy have been banished. It is in much of the imagery projected with slides onto a big screen that serves as backdrop: a view of an empty loft in which the daylight inexorably brightens and fades as Anderson plays a throbbing, ominous tune on her violin with the neon bow; refreshingly naive graphics (by Anderson herself), sophisticated yet child-like tropical islands and palm trees; shadow-animals formed with arms, hands, and fingers and cast on the screen, accompanied by "O Superman," which bring back a childhood's lost pastimes. And that disenchantment resides in the image of the performer herself, a small, detached, wistful magician emerging from the darkness into which, at evening's end, she will most certainly return—as she entered—alone.

But, perhaps most of all, the disenchanted air permeates in another powerful reminder of childhood, the highly evocative music. Much of it is disarmingly simple, often no more than electronic hums and whines and a back-and-forth alternation between two chords serving as accompaniment to the melody. Anderson favors certain types of chords—often minor seventh chords an interval away from each other, such as D minor seventh alternating with E minor seventh—that convey disenchantment, or a rising then a dying away of hope. In fact, the chords do not convey this in and of themselves. Instead—and Anderson gets a lot of mileage out of this—they evoke 60s soft-rock songs with poignant, nostalgic, lovelorn, regretful tunes, and lyrics—songs like The Drifters' "Under the Boardwalk," Mimi Fariña's guitar solo, "Miles," and America's "A Horse With No Name." If Anderson's stories and songs tell of an America that could have been a real home, her music awakens the listener's disenchantment with his own life, where he is apt to seem less at home as an adult than he did in the suburban home of his lost childhood.

In *United States, Parts 1-4,* the ultimate effect of this sort of music—which gives the opera its emotional intensity—is to make the viewer equate his or her personal disenchantment with the disenchantment he or she feels when viewing America today. Of course, the equation is a dubious one, and more poetic than objective. America is screwed up in different ways than, for instance, an individual's love affair may be. If a person does not feel at home in the United States it is not for the same reasons that he or she feels homeless on a Saturday night spent alone. Yet, the mood Anderson creates is so compelling that one winds up joining her in her wistful vision rather than saying "Hey, wait a minute, lady—you're talking about apples and oranges here, they're not the same thing!"

But *United States, Parts 1-4* also includes enchantment within the disenchantment, thanks to Anderson's bemused, funny view of technology. At one point, as she launches into another story, she uses a harmonizer to lower her voice's register to that of a nerdy middle-American male. At another, she speaks with a tiny light glowing behind her teeth so she looks lit up from within. She will speed up or slow down taped voices to comic effect. And then there are the sudden, welcome intrusions of more human sounds amidst the technology—hands clapping in time with the music, for instance, or a ghostly, wordless soprano voice that drifts through "Blue Lagoon." They add a magically tribal tone that recalls theorist Marshall McLuhan's notion of our electronic age as a return to a far more primitive one.

Further comic relief is supplied by some of the opera's satirical segments, like the one in which, with a looming Warner Brothers logo projected on the screen, Anderson reveals her technological bag of tricks to the audience. She gently pokes fun at the compromises she has to make to deal with part of corporate America—the recording industry. Her words: "And I said: Listen, I've got a vision. I see myself as part of a long tradition of American humor. You know—Bugs Bunny, Daffy Duck, Porky Pig, Elmer Fudd, Roadrunner, Yosemite Sam. And they said: 'Well, we had something a little more adult in mind.' And I said: 'OK! OK! Listen, I can adapt!' " There is biting wit in "New York Society," with its deftly sketched group portrait of art-scene types bouncing off one another at high speed as they obsessively pursue their careers. But in the end the performer leaves, vanishing into the darkness out of which she first appeared, and the audience is left with a sense of the paradoxical beauty—one that perhaps takes a certain neurotic sensibility to savor—of disappointment and loss.

Part of the delight of watching Anderson is the unlikely, but, there it is, fact that she is becoming so popular. Indeed, she was an eminently implausible candidate for superstardom. Born and raised in a well-to-do suburb outside Chicago, she began studying classical violin when she was eight, but eventually went to Barnard College in New York City to study art history. Soon she switched to a more hands-on approach to art, and started painting, sculpting, and designing graphics. At night, she taught art history in a New York City college to support herself.

Strangely enough, it was not only the growth of performance art that determined Anderson's future direction. Being a part-time academic had something to do with it, too. "I was a horrible teacher because I didn't keep up with the field and couldn't remember anything," she recalls. "So I improvised. And I found I really enjoyed being in the dark with people, talking to them and showing pictures . . ."

Anderson did not give her first performance in night school, but in downtown Manhattan. "I began playing for a small, insular community of . . . artists," she remembers. "It was very reassuring, but also very snobbish. We played for each other, and thought nobody else could really penetrate what we were doing."

In time, though, she took a determined, if unforeseen, step out of that community. Booked to perform at a Houston museum, she found the acoustics there so poor that she opted to play a funky country-western venue instead. "The regular customers were there, and so was the art world. It was a strange mix of people, but the regulars 'got' what I was doing just fine. Basically, it was fiddling and stories and film, and everyone could relate to it. They thought the way I blended this stuff was odd, but it didn't bother them." From then on, Anderson knew where she was going. "O Superman" took off and her audience grew.

Today, pop experimental musical theater is just coming into its own. Wider audiences throughout Europe, Japan, and the United States attend performances and many of the works are recorded. Incredibly, *Einstein on the Beach* was actually on the bestseller charts for classical records during its first months of release, an almost unheard-of coup for a four-record-long, avant-garde opera. Now that promoters have discovered the secret of packaging the avant-garde, exciting collaborations abound—"name" artists, fashion designers, composers, and choreographers get together to do works that draw people from all followings.

Like *Einstein on the Beach,* some of today's new musical theater eschews words and narratives, offering gestures and stage pictures in their place. In works like *Birth of a Poet* and *United States, Parts 1-4,* though, words and ideas play a more significant role. They offer a bracing change from Glass' and Monk's works, though it is hard to see how *Einstein on the Beach* or *The Games* could include coherent words or complex, developed ideas, since so much of the power in them rests on their gut-level, emotional, and spiritual appeal.

On the other hand, Anderson and Gordon (who performed with Anderson in *United*

States, Parts 1-4) compose looser, more playful music—engaging, but content to stay in the here and now rather than delve emotional depths or soar to blissful heights. It is possible that new directions in pop experimental musical theater will stem from their current work, rather than the largely non-verbal, visual musical theater of Glass and Monk. In fact, as has been noted, Glass is beginning to leave room for words and ideas more and more in his operas. All in all, this direction is an interesting one. If today's experimental musical theater proposes to help us see our world more clearly, as earlier twentieth-century experimental musical theater has, it will have to forego the obscure and the pseudo-sacred, and start learning how to—as the words on one of Laurie Anderson's favorite sweat shirts entreat—"TALK NORMAL."

Discography

Philip Glass	EINSTEIN ON THE BEACH	*CBS Masterworks M4 38875*
Philip Glass	SATYAGRAHA	*(to be released by CBS Masterworks, 1985)*
Kurt Weill	DIE DREIGROSCHENOPER	*Odyssey Y2 32977*
Laurie Anderson	UNITED STATES LIVE	*Warner Bros. 25192-1*
Meredith Monk	DOLMEN MUSIC	*ECM Records ECM-1-1197*
Meredith Monk	TURTLE DREAMS	*ECM Records ECM 1240*
Guiseppi Verdi	FALSTAFF	*Columbia D3S-750*
Richard Wagner	PARSIFAL	*Erato NUM 750105*
Virgil Thomson	FOUR SAINTS IN THREE ACTS	*Nonesuch Digital 79035*
Galt McDermott	HAIR, Original Cast Album	*RCA LSO-1150*
The Who	TOMMY	*MCA 10005*
Andrew Lloyd Webber	JESUS CHRIST SUPERSTAR, Original London Cast	*MCA-2-10000*

SOUNDS FAMILIAR

"I was composing in a minimal style in the mid-70s," recounts composer Rhys Chatham. "I mean we had so much Steve Reich and Phil Glass back then, which was wonderful, but I mean, what's a young boy to do? I needed to break out of it somehow. Along with the minimalists, I had gotten interested in world music at the time, Indian and Balinese music in particular. And I said, 'wait a minute, why not investigate our indigenous music, like jazz and rock.' I became interested in jazz for a while and then, in 1977, I heard my first Ramones concert and I said, 'This is for me.' So I picked up the electric guitar and for a year really tried to play rock, I mean, straight-ahead rock . . . After that year I thought I could keep using the context of rock while making serious music."

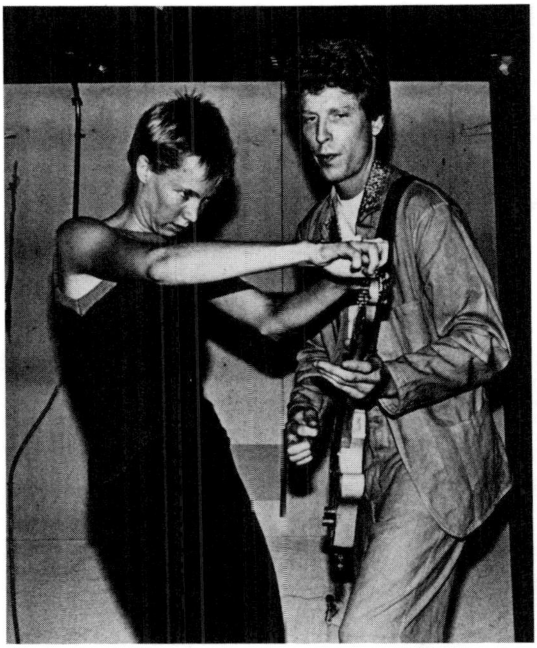
Paula Court

Rhys Chatham, who incorporates familiar rock and jazz elements into experimental sounds, performing *Drastic Classicism* with dancer Carol Armitage.

Thanks to attitudes such as Chatham's, new experimentalism sounds nowhere near as strange as it used to. Reich and Glass, realizing their personal visions in the late 60s, at first made music the likes of which no one had ever heard. Sure, they took their cue from rock and jazz, especially in the driving rhythms. But Reich's phase processes, derived from tape-loop experiments, and Glass' relentless additive structures, suggested by Indian music but completely alien to even a Punjabi ear, seemed like a complete break with both the past and the present of Western music. It created much more of a shake-up than serialism, which—even if it sounds alien to most people—is a direct descendant of the great Teutonic tradition of Western classical music. Schoenberg, after all, was following a path set by Wagner, Brahms, and Mahler, who in turn, were extending a road trod by Beethoven, Mozart, and Bach. Reich and Glass seemed to fit in nowhere. They acted like mavericks, forming their own ensembles, and sticking to their own idiosyncratic concepts.

But now Reich describes his pre-1971 music as "severe," "hard-edged," and "difficult." Indeed, despite its supremely logical and easy-to-hear structure, there was nothing familiar to it. "When you're young and you come up with something new, you're afraid that you're a lunatic. It's very reassuring to know, later, that you can be part of the globe."

There are a number of ways that pop experimental music can resemble other music, to give an audience something familiar to grasp onto. One way is for music to be written so people besides the composer's ensemble can play it. Reich's music, for instance, can now be played by standard symphony orchestras on standard programs with works by other composers. His *Variations for Winds, Strings, and Keyboards* has been double-billed with Ravel's *Bolero;* his *Tehillim* has been on programs with Ives' *Decoration Day* and Brahms' *First Symphony.* He thinks an ideal program would couple his works with the *Dance Suite* by Bartók, *Symphonies of Wind Instruments* by Stravinsky, or any baroque work, especially Bach's.

Reich now thinks that reference to the music of the past is extremely valuable. And he enjoys the fact that his recent music fits into a tradition, what he calls the French tradition of the twentieth century. "There was a fork in the road, around the turn of the century," he says. "This way to Wagner, this way to Debussy, and Copeland . . . and eventually the minimalists, and myself . . . I became more consciously aware that the things I do—for instance, repeating the notes in the middle register while changing the base notes and the harmony—are right out of *Afternoon of a Faun* [by Debussy]."

Glass, too, has begun to fit more easily into existing traditions and formats. His operas have become more and more like the traditional image of opera, and he's embarking on

Steve Reich's most recent orchestral works are closer to mainstream classical music.

Beatriz Schiller

other projects that fit within existing idioms, as well—his projected album of pop songs, for instance. And recently, younger composers, such as Rhys Chatham, Laurie Anderson, and David Van Teighem, have been making unabashed use of popular idioms, and quoting from existing pop songs.

Popular, folk, and liturgical music have been creeping into art music ever since the middle ages. Bach used the forms of seventeenth-century court dances, for his *French Suites* for harpsichord. Dvořák and Mahler incorporated folk themes in their symphonies. Stravinsky drew on Russian folk and religious music in *Les Noces,* as well as jazz in his *L'Histoire du Soldat* and *Ebony Concerto.* Kurt Weill also appropriated the forms and sounds of American jazz from the 20s in his theater music, while Darius Milhaud was inspired by the popular music of Brazil when writing his *Saudades do Brasil,* and by the New Orleans jazz he had heard for the first time in Harlem for his ballet *Le Création du Monde.*

Of course, composers who lived in such different eras as Bach, Mahler, and Stravinsky were bound to have different attitudes towards the non-art music they brought into their own compositions. Arch-individualist-against-the-world Mahler, for example, used folk tunes in an ambivalent way. He schmaltzed them up on purpose, as if to mock—and, at the same time, give himself wholly over to—the simpleminded sentiments they express. Weill, with a similarly ambivalent attitude, added wry orchestral asides and biting harmonies to the catchy vocal lines of his theater songs. Dvořák, on the other hand, as a Czech nationalist, blared forth his folk melodies with passion and sincerity. And Bach, though he did not consider his *French Suites* virtuosic enough to merit publication, brought out the emotional quality he heard in each of those courtly dances. Still, all of this music was serious music. It was accessible and familiar, yes, but still "artsy." Today's experimental music is presented in a reassuringly familiar way, much the same way as pop is presented—in clubs, with rock instruments. Even better, the music is almost—repeat almost—as undemanding as the rock music we have come to know and love.

Yet Chatham, Anderson, and Van Teighem show some of the same ambivalence towards pop that composers of the past felt. They know that rock is, in part, a packaged commodity calculated to instantly appeal to the broadest possible audience for the sake of financial gain. And Chatham, for one, says that he couldn't keep the identity of a real rocker because, "it just wasn't me." At the same time, though, the younger pop experimentalists like pop. To show their mixed feelings toward pop music, they make it wittier, drier, and more quirky than the strictly commercial stuff.

When Chatham, for example, says he uses the "context of rock," he means rock's instrumentation (electric guitars and drums, all highly amplified), its mood (anger), and its rhythms (heavy metal), as evidenced by pieces like the 1981 *Drastic Classicism.* He doesn't use the shape of a rock song—its chord progressions, chorus-and-verse structure, three-minute length—or the melodies and lyrics that one would expect in rock. Instead, he puts the rock elements into a "serious" framework, a repetitive, non-dramatic, non-melodic structure that comes directly from the minimalism of Terry Riley. In "For Brass" and other works on his 1984 LP *Factor X,* Chatham takes military marching music as his model, using fanfares of brass bands as motifs to be played in strange tunings, rearranging and repeating them as if they were short classical themes. The military and classical elements of "For Brass" are also mixed with rock elements such as a backbeat.

The use of familiar idioms can also be extended to all-embracing collage that uses not only stylistic elements of various types of music, but also actual, recognizable quotes from other types of music as well, along with experimental techniques. For instance, Charles Ives

Lisa Haun

Malcolm McLaren gathers material from all over the world and jams it together in jarring ways.

put semi-disguised snatches of hymns, minstrel songs, folk tunes, college songs, and so on into his works, perhaps most memorably in the *Symphony No. 4* and *Three Places in New England.* Apart from their nostalgic air, these tunes provided just one more thread in the dense aural fabrics of musical elements that Ives wove. His music might sound chaotic at times, with "Columbia, the Gem of the Ocean" played on the trumpets while the woodwinds shuffle and stagger downwards and the drums beat a jerky tatoo. But this is a happy chaos, one that reflects America's melting pot and democratic values, rather than a grim acceptance of entropy (the force behind chaos in nature). Likewise, Karlheinz Stockhausen's *Telemusik,* a combination and blending of folk and religious music with electronically-generated sounds, celebrates the diversity of the modern world.

Other composers are less celebratory when using diverse elements. John Cage, in the complex patchwork of disparate sounds that make up his *Fontana Mix,* conjures up a world in a state of continuing breakdown caused by cultural bombardment. In Luciano Berio's *Recital I (for Cathy),* the mad melange of musical quotes expresses the singer's nervous breakdown, which is acted out during the performance. In Berio's *Sinfonia,* though, quotes—mainly from Mahler, with bits from dozens of other composers—have a more openly nostalgic quality, one that the composer both mocks and is drawn to, in much the same way that Mahler himself mocked and loved the folk tunes he quoted in his own symphonies.

Peter Gordon, a New York-based composer now in his thirties, shows a similar ambivalence to memories of a childhood filled with rock music. He replays and distorts the old tunes with techniques from both recent experimental music and from a range of avant-garde composers, including Berio and the serialists. Gordon's surprising mixtures come partially from his knack for collaborating with numerous musicians who are composers in their own right. His Love of Life Orchestra, in fact, has included many of the musicians discussed in this book—Laurie Anderson, David Byrne, Rhys Chatham, Arto Lindsey, Kurt Munkacsi, "Blue" Gene Tyranny, and Jill Kroesen, as well as many others of varied backgrounds. "LOLO put together a framework in which all these people could play together; the music is written for particular musicians, not idealized types of musics which are then collaged."

The eclecticism of Gordon's music also comes from his own varied background. He spent a good portion of his teenage years in Munich, Germany, and studied music theory, piano, and clarinet, but also played sax with GI bands that specialized in soul music. At the same time, he listened to modernist composers such as Anton Webern and Krzysztof Penderecki and was heavily influenced by a high school teacher who was a fan of anything bohemian from Cage to Coltrane. Back in the states, he studied in music schools, then, beginning a long series of stints with rock and blues bands as a sax player, joined the L.A. rock band Little Billy and the Astros, who were often booted out of sock hops for outrageous use of synthesizers and long periods of silence. He began playing around with rock material in classical forms at a "Trust in Rock" festival at the University of California at Berkeley, which was "a populist gesture," he says, "that used the sounds and language of my contemporaries in a neo-classical way." Gordon took bits of rock and assembled them in relatively complex forms, often spicing them with acerbic harmonies.

Since Gordon founded the Love of Life Orchestra in 1977, his use of rock and other familiar material sounds less strange, with "sounds and harmonies that are right there," he says. In his "Extended Niceties," for example, he started with "a primal rock saxophone gesture," that he picked up working with rock bands. He used his obsession with the sax line "like glue" to keep a lot of different elements together. In both *Extended Niceties* and *Star Jaws,* he used standard rock structures to set up expectations that are then defied, and he also used unfamiliar devices, such as widening the distance between two voices singing in harmony.

The listener experiences these pieces as a constant, changing flow of pleasant associations from the past—a pleasantness tinged, however, with irony thanks to those defied expectations, the experimental disruptions, and the extended, repetitive structure. In Gordon's music, there's a lot of California-style soft rock that evokes drives to the beach and TV movies, and simple instrumental lines that tug at you from dozens of different nostalgic directions. There are specific associations, too, now with the 60s song "Windy", now with the theme from "Bonanza." But most of these associations remain subconscious—just as you begin to think you know what a snippet reminds you of, the music suddenly modulates around the circle of fifths, or Gordon, just as unexpectedly, gets down with a raucous, joyful sax solo straight out of today's rock 'n' roll. In making experimental music for a generation with a yearning for a continuing, idyllic childhood and a short attention span, Gordon turns the tunes of youth into a series of leitmotifs. Indeed, Theodor W. Adorno's comment about

Peter Gordon (left) with Bill T. Jones and Arnie Zane, Keith Haring, and Willie Smith in *Secret Pastures.*

Paula Court

Wagner's leitmotifs is applicable here: they serve, he says, "a commodity-function, rather like that of advertising; anticipating the universal practice of mass culture later on, the music is designed to be remembered, it is intended for the forgetful." But in helping us to remember—and altering those memories into something more pleasant than they might otherwise be—Gordon winds up with a music more intellectually stimulating than the Golden Oldies his work recycles and distorts.

In more recent works, Gordon has expanded his musical frame of reference, reprocessing, for example, elements of Verdi and combining them with atonal noise and electronic instruments (for the *Otello* of the Italian experimental theater company Falso Movimento). He describes his music for *Secret Pastures,* a 1984 collaboration with choreographers Arnie Zane and Bill T. Jones, as follows: "During 'The Announcement', a twelve-tone pitch system is used to neutralize hierarchies (tonal, textural, etc). Rigidity is offset by a syncopated rhythm and the personal taste of the composer and performers. 'The Laboratory' starts off with a tonal unison and the harmonies implied by expanding lines in contrary motion. Two melodies answer one another, a fugue evolves, things get messy." And finally, "Questions without answers. Lonely melody. The coexistence of seemingly incompatible parts." And still, the flow of familiar associations continues.

Also involved in this freewheeling collage of evocative rock styles, though perhaps in a more humorous mode, is British guitarist Fred Frith, whose songs, especially on the tour-de-force album *Cheap at Half the Price,* mixes *musique concrete* (including the voice of Ronald Reagan) with a whole gamut of identifiable rock sub-genres, from Buddy Holly to Jerry Garcia. Frith often records with a San Francisco group called The Residents, a group of anonymous collaborators with a large cult following, whose own collages use every possible pop and art music reference and range in quality from the 20-second pastiche gems of *Commercials* to the sophomoric humor of their LP *The Residents Present the Third Reich 'n' Roll.*

Recently, the use of collage and quotation has been rampant in all types of music. Part of the impetus to mix disparate music, sounds and speech comes from modern, multitrack composing, which encourages pasting together and overlaying. Discussing collage in a recent radio interview, Peter Gordon said, "I'm sure there's someone taping this show at home right now, planning to use it later in a remix with some other material." (He was right.) The result of this cavalier attitude of "Hey, let's put this together with that" is often, to say the least, disappointing, especially when the basic idea of a project is merely to slap together rock and classical material. For example, on a 1984 album produced by Philip Glass and Kurt Munkacsi, the purpose in putting the choral parts of Carl Orff's *Carmina Buvana* together with a technopop instrumental arrangement by Ray Manzarek, ex-keyboardist of the Doors, is not obvious. Instead, this attempt to enliven classical music with elements of rock seems to be a continuing mistake started in early 70s art/rock like that of Emerson, Lake and Palmer.

There is a movement now, especially among downtown New York art rockers, to use wide references to less nostalgic, less obvious, more subsumed ends. The big-band rock ensemble called the Ordinaires, for example, might be distorting movie music from spectaculars such as *Ben Hur,* but the surprises are in the quirky rhythmic and harmonic changes to the music rather than in the associations themselves.

Even more subtle is the collage David Van Teighem used as a mood-change for his *These Things Happen,* commissioned for the dance "Fait Accompli" by Twyla Tharp. Tharp gave him a tape with parts of songs by such diverse composers as Glass, Verdi, David Bowie, and Alan Vega (ex-member of Suicide). Van Teighem replaced the music of the collage with his own music, but kept the tempos and the emotional feeling of the original eclectic tape.

Ralph Records

The Residents hide their identities with sartorial savvy inspired by Rene Magritte.

Paula Court

Elliot Sharp uses a wide range of compositional techniques and instrumentations.

More ingenious still is the mixture of techniques used by composer Elliot Sharp. After a long period of using electronic music, odd tunings, noise, non-Western music, and jazz, all in a freely improvised way, Sharp, for his album *Carbon,* combined all these interests in a tight format with driving rhythms. He used the familiar rock elements in keeping with the dictum of George Clinton, the funk musician: "You get their ass in gear and their minds will follow." Sharp feels free to use any compositional technique he is interested in, as long as he does not become obsessed with it or with any one type of material. Such obsession would smack of a system, and systematic composition is the one thing he avoids most. "I always try to throw something incompatible in," says Sharp, "so there's always flukes and mutations. That's where the valuable information comes in."

All the composers mentioned so far have used a mixture of musics and techniques in order to either provide concrete contrasts of mood within a work, or to make experimental work more palatable and easy to digest so that it could be grasped by a wider audience. Sometimes, however, composers use familiar material to directly comment on that music or the culture it comes out of. Usually these comments have a negative tinge, in the form of satire or parody. This approach has its roots in the music of the early twentieth century French composer Erik Satie, who would quote "great music" (a Chopin sonata or a well-known Schubert piano piece, for example) in his own far more modest piano pieces, a context where their seriousness would sound absurd. The effect came about, in part, because of the simple music with which Satie would surround these quotations, and, in part, because of the consciously idiotic verbal asides he would stick in below the printed score.

Igor Stravinsky used musical quotations with an even nastier spirit. In his ballet score *Jeu de Cartes,* for instance, the composer would throw in bits (sometimes recognizable, sometimes cruelly exaggerated) of Rossini, Ravel, and numerous other composers, in an ironic, self-conscious manner. Such quotations were sly in-jokes for audience members who knew—just as Stravinsky knew—that "you just don't write music like those guys did anymore," at least, not in the modern world.

Today, this cynical use of quotation is found most often in rock. Sometimes, it's just a question of poking gentle fun at the never-ending stream of styles that seem to make up modern pop. At the same time, it shows up the idiocy of the planned obsolescence that keeps these things dumb, dopey, and inescapable. The B-52's, from Athens, Georgia, excel at this sort of thing, offering us the musical equivalent of Lesley Gore's flip hairdo and the vocal style Barbie and Ken would use if they could sing. The idioms of 50s and 60s rock are mixed with dissonant chords, and awkwardly-set lyrics. The crisp, clean sound lends freshness to their comments on a world that is well summed up by the changeable wigs worn by the women in the group.

The B-52's weather the fickle changes in fashion and musical style of our times.

Adrian Boot/Retna Ltd.

A darker side of rock cynicism emerges in Malcolm McLaren's *Madam Butterfly.* While the B-52's modestly limit their musical references, McLaren sticks disparate musical styles together with a flagrant disregard for history that mirrors the disregard with which this torch song's villain has treated its first-person heroine. The song—actually an aria—is "Un Bel di Vedremo," from Puccini's popular opera *Madama Butterfly.* McLaren makes the aria his song's centerpiece. Sung in an operatic soprano, it is suspended over a disco instrumental, while McLaren intones a callous monologue and a disco diva sings a modern interpretation of Butterfly's sad plight. Giving no quarter, McLaren even includes a full synopsis of the opera on the record jacket.

The long-running master of satirical rock collage is Frank Zappa. Recently, Zappa—for some incomprehensible reason—has been allowed to run amok in the sanctuaries of the high avant-garde, even getting as far as Pierre Boulez's IRCAM, the electronic music research center in Paris. The perplexing and hysterical results, as performed by the Barking Pumpkin Digital Gratification Consort and the Ensemble Intercontemporain, can be heard on the 1984 LP *The Perfect Stranger.* Music on the album parodies a gamut of twentieth-century composers, from Stravinsky, Schoenberg, and Varèse to Boulez himself, with remarkably accurate imitations that nonchalantly flow into one another. The music is accompanied by none-too-illuminating liner notes such as " 'The Girl in the Magnesium Dress' is about a girl who hates men and kills them with her special dress. Its lightweight metal construction features a lethally pointed sort of micro-Wagnerian breastplate. When they die from dancing with her, she laughs at them and wipes it off." What's really funny about this stuff is that it was actually conducted by Boulez (before, it is assumed, he saw the liner notes) in serious concerts around the world, which received appreciative reviews from classical music critics.

In pop experimentalism, then, musical quotation and collage, and other ways of toying with familiar material are used in the spirit in which Peter Gordon uses them, that is, in a friendly, though ambivalent, way. Sometimes, however, things get so friendly that the overriding effect is one of absolute reassurance. British composer Simon Jeffes, for example, with his Penguin Cafe Orchestra, puts together a wide variety of music in a way that makes them all sound like they come from one familiar source, a source close to the wellsprings of our common humanity. Jeffes, like many pop experimentalists, went through many changes in musical interest, studying classical theory early in life, going on to electronic and other avant-garde musics, and working in rock. Then he recoiled.

"In 1972," Jeffes told *New York Times* critic Stephen Holden, "I had a vivid nightmare about a bleak future in which people lived in concrete rooms where they had electronic music-making equipment and were observed by electronic surveillance. The Penguin Cafe was a fictional alternative to that alienated environment." Jeffes finds inspirational material for his soothing music in the compositions of Satie, Bach, and Beethoven, as well as African, South American, and European folk music, all combined with a touch of the pleasant side of rock. "They all seem to come from the same source because they touch you immediately," he says.

When it comes right down to it, this reassuring familiarity is a strong element of all pop experimental music, and has been from the outset. And it might explain its recent popular success. For even Glass and Reich's early music, with its "severe" structure, can be seen in this light as soothing. This is due, not only to its consonant harmonies and steady rhythms, but also to the surprisingly—and perhaps unintentionally—familiar material contained in the works. For example, with very little musical imagination, a listener can hear echoes of "Turkey in the Straw" in Part Two of Glass' *Music in Twelve Parts.* "Dance with the Dollie with a Hole in Her Pocket" echoes in both Part Nine of that same piece and in the introduction to the

Trial/Prison scene in *Einstein on the Beach.* And the main theme from the final movement of Sibelius' *Symphony No. 5* rings through "Floe" on the *Glassworks* LP. Reich too—with his frequent use of suspended ninth chords, produces the same familiar effect as Burt Bacharach did in songs like "The Look of Love" and "Knowing When to Leave."

Much has been made of the way Reich, Glass, and many other composers have achieved the impossible—creating a type of serious experimental music that reaches, and pleases, a large public. But few critics have dealt with a side of this music that is extremely problematic: that it elaborates endlessly on the givens of today's popular music—a music people today have no choice but to like, inundated with it as they are. This fact casts a shadow on the highly-touted popularity of experimental music. As German critical theorist Theodor W. Adorno claimed in his 1938 essay, "On the Fetish-Character in Music and the Regression in Listening," judgments on a piece of commercial music have nothing to do with its quality. "The familiarity of the piece," Adorno says, "is a surrogate for the quality ascribed to it. To like it is almost the same thing as to recognize it."

Equally troubling is the way critics equate pop experimentalism with more complex music, so that they snidely place the "seriousness" of pop experimental music between quotation marks. One might, however, note at least one striking difference between complex music and pop experimental music. The latter, unlike even the most compellingly rhythmic art music like Stravinsky's, for instance, relies so heavily on a regular pulse that it is bound to appeal more to the body than to the mind. In fact, it is so rhythmic that it works its way right into our bodies. It can't be listened to in a detached, objective way. The listener moves with this music; he becomes one with it, and in doing so, forgets that the composer is speaking to him through it. Complex music, whether it is by Mahler, Mozart, or Messiaen, does not allow such complete personal identification. Far richer in structure and harmonies, it is not so easy to merge with—the listener must *listen* to it. He admires it, is intrigued by it, maybe even transported—but the music remains something outside of him, something to consider rather than consume in a gulp.

Of course, the reassuringly familiar and physically compelling aspects of pop experimental music may be a hook to catch a large public and draw it in for a sophisticated musical experience. Or, it may be a hook with no meat, no substance. And yet, if nothing else, pop experimentalism has shown that not all pieces of quality music need be alike, either in the way they sound, in where and how they are presented, or what they offer to a listener. There is music meant to be considered seriously in concert halls, music meant to bliss you out, music meant to shake you up—and then there's James Brown. These kinds of music need not be interchangeable. Of course there's a breakdown of hierarchies, but hopefully, a new sense of appropriate listening has formed. Today, it would be a mistake to listen as closely to a piece meant to carry the listener into pure ecstacy as you would to, say, Olivier Messiaen's rich, multileveled *Turangalîla-Symphonie.*

With this in mind, one can imagine that in the future each type of music will have its appropriate place. For instance, you walk into an elevator and Brian Eno's *Music for Elevators* is playing. The ride up to the twenty-eighth floor is pleasant, but as you get off and go about your work, you whistle the opening measures of Philip Glass' *Pasarayam*. Later, you head down the corridor to a meeting, one of your colleagues has the latest B-52's album in tow ("I want to make a cassette for the party this weekend," she explains). An hour and a half passes—all work, no music. Later, though, your friends call to say they have gotten you a ticket for tonight's concert, featuring works by Webern, Elliot Sharp, Ives, and Boulez. You make a note not to drink too much at "happy hour," as you'll want to go to this concert clear-headed. You run into the deli downstairs, and today they've got Robert Fripp's *Music for Grocery Stores* playing. There is a splashy poster in the window announcing a local performance of a Peter Gordon "musical comedy" that looks like saucy, sexy fun. You head upstairs again, whistling Reich's fine old *Variations,* which you have been waking up to for the past month because it makes you feel so good in the morning. Then you're up and in, and sitting and working. Then you go down and out and off to the concert, slowing down to the music, pondering its secrets, buried like jewels deep inside the sounds the instruments make.

This is one scenario of how many kinds of music can fill your life. No "better" than others, no worse than most. It is something, at any rate, to play with and explore.

Discography

Claude Debussy	IMAGES	*Angel S-37066*
Rhys Chatham	FACTOR X	*Moers Music 02008*
Charles Ives	SYMPHONY NO. 4	*Columbia MS-6775*
Charles Ives	THREE PLACES IN NEW ENGLAND	*Columbia MS-6684*
Luciano Berio	SIN FONIA	*Columbia MS-7268*
Peter Gordon	STAR JAWS	*Lovely Music 1031*
Fred Frith	CHEAP AT HALF THE PRICE	*Ralph Records 8356*
The Residents	COMMERCIALS	*Ralph Records 8052*
David Van Teighem	THESE THINGS HAPPEN	*Warner Bros. 9-25105-1*
Elliot Sharp	CARBON	*Zoar 15*
Igor Stravinsky	JEU DE CARTES	*Deutsche Grammophon DG 2530537*
The B-52's	THE B-52's	*BSK 3355*
Malcolm McLaren	MADAM BUTTERFLY	*Island 0-96915*
Frank Zappa conducted by Pierre Boulez	THE PERFECT STRANGER	*Angel DS-38170*
Penguin Cafe Orchestra	BROADCASTING FROM HOME	*Editions EG EGED 39*

BIBLIOGRAPHY

Anderson, Laurie, *United States.* New York: Harper & Row, 1984.

Appleton, John N., and **Ronald C. Perera,** eds. *The Development and Practice of Electronic Music.* Englewood Cliffs, New Jersey: Prentice-Hall, 1975.

Baker, Rob. "Talking Heads Get Metaphysical." *Daily News,* 12 June 1983.

Banes, Sally. *Terpsichore in Sneakers: Post Modern Dance.* Boston: Houghton-Mifflin Company, 1980.

Bersani, Leo. *A Future for Astyanax.* Boston and Toronto: Little, Brown & Company, 1976.

Brewster, Todd. "Portrait: Philip Glass." *Life,* August 1981.

Brown, Peter, and **Steven Gaines.** *The Love You Make: An Insider's Story of the Beatles.* New York: McGraw-Hill Book Company, 1983.

Cage, John. *Silence.* Cambridge, Massachusetts and London: M.I.T. Press, 1961.

Carr, Tim. *"That Downtown Sound . . . From A to Z." New York Rocker,* June 1982.

Chernoff, John Miller. *African Rhythm and African Sensibility.* Chicago and London: University of Chicago Press, 1979.

Cocks, Jay. "Sing a Song of Seeing." *Time,* 26 December 1983: 54-64.

Coupe, Stuart, and **Glenn A. Baker.** *The New Rock 'n' Roll.* New York: St. Martin's Press, 1983.

Cowell, Henry, and **Sidney Cowell.** *Charles Ives and His Music.* New York and London: Oxford University Press, 1955.

De Jong, Constance, and **Philip Glass.** *Satyagraha: M.K. Gandhi in South Africa, 1893-1914.* New York: Standard Editions, 1980.

Emerson, Ken. "Rock: Talking Heads Enter the Mainstream." *New York Times,* 24 January 1979.

Ewen, David. *Composers of Tomorrow's Music.* New York: Dodd, Mead, & Company, 1971.

Frith, Simon. *Sound Effects: Youth, Leisure, and the Politics of Rock 'n' Roll.* London: Pantheon, 1981.

Glass, Philip. "Interview." *Semiotexte* 3, no. 2 (1978).

Goldman, Albert. *Freakshow.* New York: Atheneum, 1971.

Graustark, Barbara. "Cross-Cultural Encounter." *Newsweek,* 15 December 1980.

Griffiths, Paul. *Modern Music: The Avant-Garde Since 1945.* New York: George Braziller, 1981.

"The Heart Is Back in the Game." *Time,* 20 September 1982.

Holden, Stephen. "A Hoedown from Britain Mixing Folk and Classical." *New York Times,* 7 December 1984.

"Hollywood Catches the Rock Beat." *Time,* 26 March 1984.

Kardon, Janet. *Laurie Anderson: Works From 1969 to 1982.* Philadelphia: Institute of Contemporary Art, University of Pennsylvania, 1983.

Kroll, Jack. "An Electronic Cassandra." *Newsweek,* 21 February 1983.

Levy, Stephen. "Ad Nauseum: How MTV Sells Out Rock 'n' Roll." *Rolling Stone,* 8 December 1983.

Maconie, Robin. *The Works of Karlheinz Stockhausen.* London and Boston: Marion Boyars, 1976.

Mellers, Wilfrid. *Twilight of the Gods.* New York: Viking Press; London: Faber, 1973.

Mertens, Wim. *American Minimal Music.* London: Kahn & Averil; New York: Alexander Broude Inc., 1983.

Miller, Jim. "The Wizards of Sound." *Newsweek,* 10 September 1984.

Newman, Charles. "The Post-Modern Aura: The Act of Fiction in an Age of Inflation." *Salmagundi,* nos. 63-64 (Spring–Summer 1984).

Norman, Philip. *Shout!: The Beatles in Their Generation.* New York: Simon & Schuster; London: Elmtree and Corgi, 1981.

O'Brian, Glenn, and **Robert Becker.** "Laurie Anderson." *Interview,* December 1984.

Pareles, Jon. "Talking Heads in Motion." *Village Voice,* 22 October 1980.

Reich, Steve. *Writings About Music.* Halifax: The Press of the Nova Scotia College of Art and Design; New York: New York University Press, 1974.

Roberts, John Storm. *Black Music of Two Worlds.* New York: William Morrow & Company, 1974.

Rockwell, John. *All American Music.* New York: Alfred A. Knopf, 1983.

Rockwell, John. "The Artistic Success of Talking Heads." *New York Times,* 11 September 1977. "New Territory for Talking Heads." *The New York*

Times, October 5, 1980. "Talking Heads: Cool in the Glare of Hot Rock." *New York Times,* 24 March 1976.

Rudhyar, Dane. *The Magic of Tone and the Art of Music.* Boulder, Colorado and London: Shambala, 1982.

Sandow, Gregory. "Alarm Clocks and Lullabies." *Village Voice,* 9 November 1982.

Schwarz, Robert K. "From Minimal to Maximal: Steve Reich and *The Desert Music.*" *On the Next Wave* 2, nos. 1-2, (October 1984).

Schwartz, Tony. "Straight Talk." *Newsweek,* 21 August 1978.

Schweitzer, Albert. *J.S. Bach.* New York: Macmillan Company, 1911.

Sennett, Richard. "Twilight of the Tenured Composer." *Harper's* December 1984.

Shewey, Don. "The Performing Artistry of Laurie Anderson." *New York Times Magazine,* 6 February 1983.

Sterritt, David. "Laurie Anderson . . . ." *The Christian Science Monitor,* 24 October 1983.

This Fabulous Century, Vol VII: 1960-1970. New York: Time-Life Books, 1970.

Vlad, Roman. *Stravinsky.* London and New York: Oxford University Press, 1978.

Walsh, Michael. "Switched-On Rock, Wired Classics." *Time,* 27 February 1984. "Post-Punk Apocalypse." *Time,* 21 February 1983.

INDEX

A

Acker, Kathy, 92
Adam and the Ants, 17
Adams, John, 83
Adé, King Sunny, x, 16
Adorno, Theodor W., 103, 106, 111
African Beats, the, x
African music, ix, 6, 7, 8, 10, 12, 15, 16, 17, 23, 56, 110
Akalaitis, Joanne, 86
Alvin, Juliette, 17
Amacher, Maryanne, 65
ambient music, 73–75
amplification, effect of, xii, 22–23
Anderson, Laurie, x, xii, 27, 61, *76*, *94–95*, 101–3; and opera, 83, 93, 96–97, 98; and technology, 44, 53, 57, 60; and video, 71, 72
Ant, Adam, 17
Antheil, George, 21, 43
anti-art, 36, 80
Arabic music, 36
Art of Noise, 60
Artaud, Antonin, 80
Artistics, the, 13
Ashford and Simpson, 16
Ashley, Robert, 22, 27, *62–63;* and video opera, 61, 71–72, 75
atonal music, xiii. *See also* serial music
Aunt Jemima and the United Pancakes, 40

B

Babbitt, Milton, 11, 50
Bach, Johann Sebastian, xii, 20, 50, 99, 100, 101, 110
Bacon, Francis, 20
Bacharach, Burt, 111
Balinese music, 6, 8, 18, 99
Ball, Hugo, 16
Bambaataa, Afrika, 53, *54–55*, 60
Barking Pumpkin Digital Gratification Consort, the, 110
Bartok, Bela, xvii, 100
Beatles, the, xx–xxi, *xxii*, xxiv, 1, 17, 18
Beck, Jeff, 27
Beethoven, Ludwig Van, 32, 99, 110
Benjamin, Walter, 69
Berberian, Cathy, 37
Berg, Alban, xiii, 37
Berio, Luciano, 21, 22, 37, 50, 102–103, 112
Berlioz, Hector, 77
Bernstein, Leonard, 12
Bersani, Leo, 83
B–52's, the, *109*, 109–10, 112
Big Brother and the Holding Company, xxi
Black Flag, 32, 43
blues, the, x, xx, xxii, 23–24, 37, 40, 103
Boulanger, Nadia, 3
Boulez, Pierre, xiii–xiv, 46, 110, 112
Bow Wow Wow, 17
Bowie, David, 74, 81, 86, 106
Brahms, Johannes, 99, 100
Branca, Glenn, 32–35, *33*, 43, 56, 61, 65, 82, 83
Brazilian music, 101
Brecht, Bertolt, 81
Breuer, Lee, 83
British Invasion, xx, xxiii, 23
Bronski Beat, the, 17
Brooklyn Academy of Music, The (BAM), 83, 86
Brooks, Conrad, 6
Brown, James, 15, 18
Bryars, Gavin, 74
Buchwalter, Steven, 57
Budd, Harold, 12, 17, 74, 75
Buzzcocks, the, 32
Byrd Hoffmann School of Byrds, the, 76
Byrne, David, *14–15*, 27, 40, 43, 103; and environmental music, 69–70; and non-Western music, 13, 16; and opera, 87; and video, 72

C

Cage, John, xv, *xviii–xix*, xxiv, 18, *22*, 22 43, 74; and collage, 102; and electronic music, 50; and environmental music, 69, 73; noise pieces of, 21–22; and non-Western music, 7, 8
Cale, John, xxiii
capitalism, influence of, xx, 1, 3, 46, 56, 82, 97
Captain Beefheart (Don Van Vliet), xxiii
Cardew, Cornelius, 17, 74
Carlos, Walter, 50, 60
Carr, Tim, 32
Carter, Elliott, xiii, 11
CBGB's, 13, 27, 32, 35, 65, *66–67*
Chatham, Rhys, 35, 64–65, *99*, 99 101, 103, 112
Chernoff, John Miller, xx
Childs, Lucinda, 76, 77
Chong, Ping, 83, 90, 91–92
Chopin, Frederic, 109
Christian, Charlie, 23
Clapton, Eric, 27
Clash, the, 32
Clinton, George, 108
Cocks, Jay, 71
collage, musical, xxi, xxiii, 45, 53, 101–11
Collapsing New Buildings, 37, *38–39*
Columbia–Princeton Electronic Music Center, *47*, 47–48, 60
Como, Perry, 40
computers, use of, xii, 44, 45, 46, 51, 56–57
Cooper, Alice, 81–82
Copeland, Aaron, xxiii, 3, 100
Cream, 27
Crickets, the, 23
Crumb, George, 22
Crystals, the, 45
Culture Club, 17

D

Damned, the, 32
dance, xvii, 8, 32, 40, 51, 53, 91
Danceteria, 65, *68*
Davidovsky, Mario, *47*
Davies, Hunter, xxi
Davis, Miles, 13
Debussy, Claude, 7, 100, 112
de Jong, Constance, 86
Depeche Mode, 17
Dessau, Paul, 81
Deuter, 12, 74
Devo, 74
Dewys, Margaret, 34
Diaghilev, Serge, xvii
Diddley, Bo, 23
disco, 51, 110
DNA, 35, *36*, 43
Dodd, Coxone, 45
Dolby, Thomas, 51
Doors, the, 1, 106
Douglas, Mary, 8
Dvořak, Antonin, 101

E

Eastern philosophy. *See* religious influences
Eisler, Hanns, 81
Electric Circus, the, xxi,
electronic music, ix, xii, xxiii, 45–53, 56, 57, 60, 108, 110
Emerson, Lake and Palmer, 51, 81
Emmel, Felix, 42–43
Eno, Brian, x, xii, 27, *44*, 111; and ambient music, 72–74, 75; and Talking Heads, 16
Ensemble Intercontemporain, the, 110
environmental music, 69–75
Eurythmics, 51, *52*
Exploding Plastic Inevitable, xxiii

Ewen, David, xi

F
Fabian, 45
Faithful, Marianne, xxi
Falso Movimento, 106
Fariña, Mimi, 96
Fela, 16
Fender, Leo, 23
Ferry, Bryan, 74
Fitzgerald, Kit, 72
Five Blind Boys of Alabama, the, 83
Fluxus, 69
folk music, 101, 102, 103, 110
Foreman, Richard, 92
Foster, Stephen, xiv
Frankie Goes to Hollywood, 53
Frantz, Chris, 13, 15, 16
Freed, Allan, xv
Freud, Sigmund, xiii, 37, 87
Friedman, Bruce Jay, 69
Fripp, Robert, 74, 112
Frith, Fred, 106, 112
furniture music, 68, 73
Futurism, 21, 37, 53, 80

G
Gabriel, Peter, 51
Galas, Diamanda, *42*, 42, 43
Gandhi, Mohandas K., 86
Gang of Four, 37
Garcia, Jerry, 106
George, Boy, 17
Gibson, Jon, 65
Glass, Philip, *4–5*, 40, *58–59*, 64–65, 70, *78–79*, *88–89*, 106; and non-Western music, 3–6, 7, 8, 10–12, 13, 15, 16, 17, 18; and opera, 76–77, 80, 82, 83, 86–87, 90, 97–98; and pop music, ix, xii, xv, xvii, 99, 100–1, 110–11; and technology, 56–57; and video, 72,75
Gluck, Christoph W., 7
Goldman, Albert, 37, 82
Gordon, David, 91
Gordon, Peter, 27, 103, *104–105*, 106, 110, 112; and opera, 83, 92, 98; and video, 72
Grandmaster Flash, 51, 53, 60
Grant, Linda, *28*
Grateful Dead, the, xxi
Grotowski, Jerzy, 80, 83
guitar armies, 34

H
Hancock, Herbie, 53
Hari, Chaitanya, 12
Haring, Keith, *104–105*
Harmonic Choir, the, 13, 18
Harrison, George, xx, 1, *3*
Harrison, Jerry, 13, 16, 70
Harrison, Lou, 7, 8
Harry, Debbie, 65
Hassell, Jon, 12–13, 16, 17, 18
Hebrew music, 6, 11, 56
Hendrix, Jimi, xxii, 27, *29*, 37, 43
Henry, Pierre, 46
Hesse, Hermann, xxi, xxiv
hip-hop music, 53
Holden, Stephen, 110
Holly, Buddy, 23, 106
Horn, Trevor, 53, 60
House, the, 91
Human League, the, 51
Hüsker Dü, 32
Hykes, David, 13, 16, 17, 18, 35

I
Indian music, 6, 7, 8, 10, 12, 13, 99; and rock music, xx, 1, 8, 17, 26
Indonesian influences, 7, 56, 81. *See also* Balinese music
industrial rock, 37
Isozaki, Arata, 13
Ives, Charles, *xi*, xiv–xv, xxi, xxiv, 100, 101–2, 112
Ives, George, xiv

J
Jagger, Mick, xxi
Janàček, Leos, xvii, xx
Japanese theater, 81
Jarre, Jean-Michel, 51, 60
Javanese music, 7
jazz, 6, 7, 13, 23, 99, 101, 108
Jefferson Airplane, the, xxi, 36
Jeffes, Simon, 110
Jones, A.M., 6
Jones, Bill T., 72, *104–105*, 106
Joplin, Janis, 40

K
Karpath, Ludwig, xiii
Khan, Ali Akbar, 1
Khan, Ulan, 1
Killing Joke, 51
Kinks, the, 27
Kitaro, 12, 74
Kitchen, the, *61*, 64
Kraftwerk, 51, 53
Kramer, Jack, 27
Kreiger, Arthur, *47*
Kroesen, Jill, 71, 103

L
LaBarbara, Joan, 42
Labelle, 16
Leary, Timothy, 3
Lennon, John, xxi, *3*, 69, 74
Lennox, Annie, 51, *52*,
Lessing, Doris, 87
Lewis, Jerry Lee, 45
Lichtenstein, Harvey, 83, 86
Ligeti, Gyorgy, 21
Limbo Lounge, the, 65
Lindsey, Arto, 35, *36*, 103
Little Billy and the Astros, 103
Little Richard, 23
Live Skull, 36, 37
Living Theater, the, 83
Lohn, Jeffrey, 34
Love of Life Orchestra, the, 27, 103
LSD, xxi, 3, 81
Lucier, Alvin, 22, *24–25*
Luening, Otto, 50
Lunch, Lydia, 35, 43
Lydon, Johnny, 36
Lyotard, Jean-Francois, 17

M
Mabou Mines, the, 86
Maharishi Mahesh Yogi, 1, 3
Mahavishnu Orchestra, 8, *9*, 18
Mahler, Gustav, xii, 20, 32, 101, 103,111
Mailer, Norman, 27
Manzanera, Phil, 74
Manzarek, Ray, 106
Marley, Bob, and the Wailers, 60
marijuana, xxi
Martin, George, xx, xxi
Material, 53
Max's Kansas City, 34, 65
McCartney, Paul, xx
McDermott, Galt, 98
MC5, 27
McLaren, Malcolm, x, 17, 27, 32, 53, *102*, 110, 112
McLaughlin, John, *9*. *See also* Mahavishnu Orchestra
McLuhan, Marshall, xxiv,. 96
Mellers, Wilfrid, 8
Mertens, Wim, 17
Messiaen, Olivier, 7, 8, 18, 111
Milhaud, Darius, xvii, 68, 73, 101
military marching music, xiv–xv, 101
Mimoroglu, Ilhan, 50
minimalism, xii, 10, 11–12, 22, 69, 83, 99, 100, 101; and rock music, xxiii, 15, 32, 35
Miyake, Issey, 13
Moby Grape, xxi
Mongolian music, 13
Monk, Meredith, xii, *41*, 72, *73*, 75, *90*; and musical theater, 82, 83, 91–92, 97, 98; and vocal style, 40, 42, 43
Monsoon, 17
Moog, Robert, 50
Moorman, Charlotte, 27
Moran, Robert, 87
Moroccan music, 6, 8
Moroder, Giorgio, 51
Mozart, Wolfgang Amadeus, 7, 64, 82, 98, 111
MTV, 71
Mudd Club, the, 65
multitracking technology. *See* recording technology
Munkacsi, Kurt, 56–57, 103, 106
Murray the K, 61
Music Electronica Viva, 65

musique concrete, xxi, 45–46, 50, 53, 106. *See also* collage, musical
Muzak, 68–69, 72–73
Myers, Rollo, 68

N
Nancarrow, Conlon, 46, 60
Nath, Pandit Pran, 7, 13
Neuhaus, Max, 69
New Age music, 12, 51, 74
New Wave music, xxiii, 51, 65
New York Dolls, the, xxiii, 27
Niblock, Phil, 65
noise, extra-musical, xv, xxiii, 20–23, 26–27, 32, 34–37, 108
noise rock, xxiii, 32, 35, 65, 92
non-Western music, xii, xxiv, 1–18, 108. *See also* African music; Arabic music; Balinese music; Brazilian music; Hebrew music; Indian music; Indonesian influences; Javanese music; Mongolian music; Moroccan music; South American music; Yemenite music
Nylon, Judy, 73

O
O'Brien, Joe, 69
Ono, Yoko, 42, 69
opera, xii, 71, 75, 76–81, 82–98, 100
Ordinaires, the, 106
Oregon, 8
Orff, Carl, 7, 8, 81, 106
Ouellete, Fernand, 50

P
Page, Jimmy, 27
Pain, Tom, 36
Parliament–Funkadelic, 16
Partch, Harry, 7, 8, 21–22
Paul, Les, 23, 45
Penderecki, Krysztof, 21, 37, 40, 103
Penguin Cafe Orchestra, the, 110, 112
performance art, 81, 97
Perry, Lee, 45
phase music, 6, 53, 56, 99
Phillips, Sam, 45
Plank, Connie, 51
Poison–Tête, Victor, 37
Police, the, 86
Presley, Elvis, xx, 45
Preston, Robert, 40
Procol Harum, 51
Prokofiev, Serge, xvii
psychedelic rock, xxi–xxii, xxiv, 1, 40, 51
Public Image Ltd., 36, 43
Puccini, Giacomo, 20, 110
punk music, xxiii, 30–31, 32, 65
Pyramid Club, the, 65

Q
Quicksilver Messenger Service, xxi
quotation, musical, 101–2, 103, 106, 109–10. *See also* collage, musical

R
Ramones, the, xxiii, 27, 43, 65, 99
rap music, 53
Rat At Rat R, 37
Ravel, Maurice, 100, 109
Ray, Johnny, xx
Reagan, Ronald, 106
recording technology, ix, xii, xx–xxi, 44–46, 47, 51, 53, 56–57, 74, 106
reggae, 45
Reggio, Godfrey, 72
Reich, Steve, xii, *1*, 26–27, 83, *100*; and non-Western music, 6, 7, 8, 10, 11, 12, 13, 15, 16, 17, 18; and phase music, 53, 56, 60; and popular music, xvii, 99, 100, 110–11; and venues, 61, 65; and vocal style, 40
Reisman, Michael, 57
religious influences, xxiv, 1, 3, 7, 8, 11, 13, 16, 17–18, 22, 35, 68, 74, 86
Residents, the, 106, *107*, 112
Riley, Terry, 6–7, 8, 10, 11, 12, 16, 17, 18, 35, 53, 101
Rimsky–Korsakov, Nikolai, 7
Roberts, John Storm, 23
rock music, ix, xi–xii, xv, xx–xxi, 99, 101, 103–8, 110, 111; and electronic music, 51, 53; as environmental music, 69–70; and instrumental experimentation, 23, 26–27, 32, 34–37; and non-Western music, 1, 3, 8, 13–18; and quotation and collage, 103–8, 109–10, 111; and recording technology, 44, 45; in theater, 81–82, 86, 96; and video, 71, 72, 74–75; and vocal style, 40
Rockwell, John, 14, 22
Roedelius, Hans–Joachim, 12, 74
Rolling Stones, the, ix, x, xx, xxi, 1, 23, 27, 45
Rorem, Ned, xii
Rosenfeld, Paul, 21
Rossini, Giaocchino, 109
Rotten, Johnny, 36
Roundhouse, the, 64
Roxy Music, 74
Rubin, William, 17
Rudhyar, Dane, 34–35
Russollo, Luigi, 21
Rzewski, Frederick, 65

S
Salle, David, 92
Sanborn, John, 19, 71
Sandow, Gregory, 13
Satie, Erik, 21, 43, 68, 73, 75
Sax, Adolphe, 20
Schaeffer, Pierre, 45–46, 51
Schoenberg, Arnold, xiii, xv, xxiv, 11, 20, 21, 37, 43, 99, 110
Schubert, Franz, 109
Scriabin, Alexander, 68
Second Viennese School, xi
Sellars, Peter, 13, 83
serial music, xiii–xiv, xv, xxiv, 3, 8, 11, 99, 103
Sex Pistols, the, xxiii, 17, 27, 32, 36
Shankar, Ravi, 1, *2*, 3, 6
Shankar, Ude, 1
Shapiro, David, 77
Sharp, Elliot, *108*, 108, 112
Shriek Opera, 43
Shuller, Gunther, 6
Sibelius, Jean, 111
Simon, Paul, xii
Sinatra, Frank, 40
Sixties, the, xx, 65, 86
Slits, the, 32
Smiley, Pril, *47*
Smith, Willie, *104–105*
Sonic Youth, 37, 43
sound–color music, 20–23
South American music, 110
South Bronx, 51
Spector, Phil, 45, 60
Speigel, Laurie, 65
Stalin, Joseph, 77
Static, the, 34
Stein, Gertrude, 82–83
Stewart, Dave, 51, *52*
Stockhausen, Karlheinz: and electronic music, 50, 60, 102; and environmental music, 69; and instrumental experimentation, 21, 22; and serial music, xiii–xiv, 13; and vocal style, 37, 40
Stravinsky, Igor, *xvii*, xvii, xx, xxiv, 20, 100, 101, 109, 110, 112
Subotnick, Morton, 26
Sugarhill Gang, the, 53
Suicide, 106
Summers, Andy, 86
Sutton, Sheryl, 76
Suzuki, D.K., 1
Swans, 37
synthetic music. *See* electronic music

T
Talking Heads, ix, xii, 13–16, *14–15*, 17, 18, 69–70, 71, 74, 87
Tchaikovsky, Peter I., 20
technology, effect of, ix, xii, xxi, xxiv, 44–60, 96. *See also* amplification; collage, musical; electronic

music; recording technology; video
Teenage Jesus and the Jerks, 35
Television, xxiii, 65
Test Department, 37
theater, musical, xxi, xxii, 32, 76–98. *See also* opera
Theoretical Girls, 34
Thomson, Virgil, 3, 83, 98
Tilson, Bob, 83
Tom Tom Club, the, 16, 70
Tomita, Isao, 51
Townshend, Peter, xxi, 74, 81
twelve-tone music. *See* serial music
Tharp, Twyla, 106
Tynan, Kenneth, xxi
Tyranny, "Blue" Gene, 71, 103

U
Ultravox, 51
United States (band), xxiv
Ussachevsky, Vladimir, 50

V
Van Teighem, David, *19*, 19, 26–27, 43, 56, 60, 71, 101, 106, 108, 112
Vangelis, *48–49*, 51, 60
Varèse, Edgard, *xvi*; and electronic music, 46, 50, 110; and noise, xv, xxiii, 21, 22, 26, 43
Vasulka, Steina and Woody, 64
Vega, Alan, 106
Velvet Underground, the, xxiii, xxiv, 27
venues, 11, 61, 64–65, 101
Verdi, Giuseppe, 20, 82, 98, 106
Vibrators, the, 32
video, xii, 65, 71–72, 74–75
vocal style, 37, 40, 42, 43, 75
Vollenweider, Andreas, 74

W
Wagner, Richard, xiii, 80, 98, 99, 100, 106
Walker, T-Bone, 23
Warhol, Andy, xxiii, 83
Webber, Andrew Lloyd, 98
Webern, Anton, xiii, 21, 64, 103
Weill, Kurt, 81, 98, 101
Weymouth, Tina, 13, 14, 16
White, Josh, 71
Who, the, xxi, 27, 81, 82, 98
Wilson, Robert, 76–80, *78–79*, 81, 82–83, *84–85*, 87
Win, Annabella Lu, 17
Wischerth, Stephen, 34
Wray, Link, 23

X
Xenakis, Iannis, xxiii, 50
XTC, 17

Y
Yardbirds, the, 27
Yemenite music, 6
Yes, 51, 53
Young, LaMonte, xxiii, 6–7, 8, 13, 22, 35, 65, 69
Young, Percy M., 69

Z
Zane, Arnie, 72, *104–105*, 106
Zappa, Frank, xxiii, 26, 110, 112
Z'ev, 34
Zorn, John, *26*
Zulu Nation, 53
Zvonar, Richard, 43